OXFORD WORLD'S CLASSICS

TWILIGHT OF THE IDOLS

FRIEDRICH NIETZSCHE (1844–1900) was born in Röcken, Saxony, and educated at the universities of Bonn and Leipzig. At the age of only 24 he was appointed Professor of Classical Philology at the University of Basle, but prolonged bouts of ill health forced him to resign from his post in 1879. Over the next decade he shuttled between the Swiss Alps and the Mediterranean coast, devoting himself entirely to thinking and writing. His early books and pamphlets (*The Birth of Tragedy*, *Untimely Meditations*) were heavily influenced by Wagner and Schopenhauer, but from *Human, All Too Human* (1878) on, his thought began to develop more independently, and he published a series of ground-breaking philosophical works (*The Gay Science*, *Thus Spake Zarathustra*, *Beyond Good and Evil*, *On the Genealogy of Morals*) which culminated in a frenzy of production in the closing months of 1888. In January 1889 Nietzsche suffered a mental breakdown from which he was never to recover, and he died in Weimar eleven years later. *Twilight of the Idols* (1888) is a wide-ranging critique of European philosophical and cultural values which provides a highly entertaining overview of his themes and styles.

DUNCAN LARGE is Lecturer in German at University of Wales Swansea, and Chairman of the Friedrich Nietzsche Society. He has translated Sarah Kofman's *Nietzsche and Metaphor* (1993) and is also translating Nietzsche's *Ecce Homo* for Oxford World's Classics.

OXFORD WORLD'S CLASSICS

For almost 100 years Oxford World's Classics have brought readers closer to the world's great literature. Now with over 700 titles—from the 4,000-year-old myths of Mesopotamia to the twentieth century's greatest novels—the series makes available lesser-known as well as celebrated writing.

The pocket-sized hardbacks of the early years contained introductions by Virginia Woolf, T. S. Eliot, Graham Greene, and other literary figures which enriched the experience of reading. Today the series is recognized for its fine scholarship and reliability in texts that span world literature, drama and poetry, religion, philosophy and politics. Each edition includes perceptive commentary and essential background information to meet the changing needs of readers.

OXFORD WORLD'S CLASSICS

══

FRIEDRICH NIETZSCHE

Twilight of the Idols

or

How to Philosophize with a Hammer

══

Translated with an Introduction and Notes by
DUNCAN LARGE

Oxford   New York
OXFORD UNIVERSITY PRESS

Oxford University Press, Great Clarendon Street, Oxford OX2 6DP

Oxford New York

Athens Auckland Bangkok Bogotá Buenos Aires Calcutta
Cape Town Chennai Dar es Salaam Delhi Florence Hong Kong Istanbul
Karachi Kuala Lumpur Madrid Melbourne Mexico City Mumbai
Nairobi Paris São Paulo Singapore Taipei Tokyo Toronto Warsaw
and associated companies in Berlin Ibadan

Oxford is a registered trade mark of Oxford University Press

First published as a World's Classics paperback 1998
Reissued as an Oxford World's Classics paperback 1998

British Library Cataloguing in Publication Data

Data available

Library of Congress Cataloging in Publication Data
Nietzsche, Friedrich Wilhelm, 1844–1900.
[Götzendämmerung. English]
Twilight of the idols, or, How to philosophize with a hammer /
Friedrich Nietzsche; translated with an introduction and notes by
Duncan Large.
Includes bibliographical references and index.
1. Philosophy. I. Large, Duncan. II. Title.
B3313.G6713 1998 1793—dc21 97–28215
ISBN 0–19–283138–0 (pbk.)

3 5 7 9 10 8 6 4 2

Typeset by Pure Tech India Ltd., Pondicherry
Printed in Great Britain by
Cox & Wyman Ltd.
Reading, Berkshire

CONTENTS

ABBREVIATIONS

Cross-references within *Twilight of the Idols* are by paragraph number. References to Nietzsche's other works are also by paragraph number, except for the correspondence and the unpublished notes not collected in *The Will to Power*, where volume and page references to the German editions are given. The following are the abbreviations used and the editions from which illustrative quotations have been taken:

AC   *The Antichrist* (1888), in *Twilight of the Idols and The Anti-Christ*, trans. R. J. Hollingdale (Harmondsworth: Penguin, 1968).

BGE   *Beyond Good and Evil* (1886), trans. R. J. Hollingdale (Harmondsworth: Penguin, 1973).

BT   *The Birth of Tragedy* (1872), in *The Birth of Tragedy and The Case of Wagner*, trans. Walter Kaufmann (New York: Vintage, 1967).

D   *Daybreak* (1881), trans. R. J. Hollingdale (Cambridge: Cambridge University Press, 1982).

EH   *Ecce Homo* (1888), trans. R. J. Hollingdale, 2nd edn. (Harmondsworth: Penguin, 1992).

GM   *On the Genealogy of Morals* (1887), trans. Douglas Smith (Oxford: Oxford University Press, 1996).

GS   *The Gay Science* (1882–7), trans. Walter Kaufmann (New York: Vintage, 1974).

HA   *Human, All Too Human* (1878–80), trans. R. J. Hollingdale (Cambridge: Cambridge University Press, 1986).

KGB   *Nietzsche Briefwechsel. Kritische Gesamtausgabe*, ed. Giorgio Colli and Mazzino Montinari, 16 vols. (Berlin and New York: de Gruyter, 1975–84).

KGW   *Nietzsche Werke. Kritische Gesamtausgabe*, ed. Giorgio Colli and Mazzino Montinari, 30 vols. (Berlin and New York: de Gruyter, 1967–   ).

KSA   *Friedrich Nietzsche: Sämtliche Werke. Kritische Studienausgabe in 15 Bänden*, 2nd edn., ed. Giorgio Colli and Mazzino Montinari (Munich: dtv; Berlin and New York: de Gruyter, 1988).

NcW   *Nietzsche contra Wagner* (1888), in *The Portable Nietzsche*, ed. and trans. Walter Kaufmann (New York: Viking Penguin, 1976), 661–83.

UM   *Untimely Meditations* (1873–6), trans. R. J. Hollingdale (Cambridge: Cambridge University Press, 1983).

WC *The Wagner Case* (1888), in *The Birth of Tragedy and The Case of Wagner*, trans. Walter Kaufmann (New York: Vintage, 1967).

WP *The Will to Power*, trans. Walter Kaufmann and R. J. Hollingdale (New York: Vintage, 1968).

Z *Thus Spake Zarathustra* (1883–5), trans. R. J. Hollingdale as *Thus Spoke Zarathustra* (Harmondsworth: Penguin, 1961).

INTRODUCTION

This work of not even 150 pages, cheerful and fateful in tone, a demon that laughs—the product of so few days that I hesitate to say how many— is the absolute exception among books: there is nothing richer in substance, more independent, more subversive—more wicked. Anyone who wants to get a quick idea of how topsy-turvy everything was before I came along should make a start with this work. What the title-page calls *idol* is quite simply what till now has been called truth. *Twilight of the Idols*—in plain words: the old truth is coming to an end... (EH III 'TI' 1)

So begins Nietzsche's own unabashed appraisal of *Twilight of the Idols* in a typically hyperbolic passage from his late autobiographical text *Ecce Homo*, and indeed in a number of respects it is undeniably an exceptional work. The first draft was composed in just over a week, between 26 August and 3 September 1888, while Nietzsche was staying at his customary summer haunt of Sils-Maria in the Upper Engadine, and this was a notable feat even by the standards of that astonishingly productive last year in his mentally active life, a year which saw him complete no fewer than six separate texts. As is evident from this passage, Nietzsche himself intended *Twilight* to serve as a short introduction to the whole of his philosophy, and consequently it is also the most synoptic of his books: it can be comfortably read in one or two sittings and recommends itself as giving the best single-volume overview of Nietzsche's mature philosophical themes and styles, even if its lapidary concision makes it at the same time the most condensed and allusive of all his works. 'My ambition', he tells us here, 'is to say in ten sentences what everyone else says in a book—what everyone else does *not* say in a book...' (IX 51). No sooner had he received his first printed copies of the work, in November 1888, than he began looking to have it translated into other languages, for he fully expected it to have an impact and to gain him the wider readership which had so far eluded him. One can easily see why: it is a book he greatly enjoyed writing, and his style is such that that enjoyment—the sheer delight he takes in his own 'demonic' mischief-making, in parading his

philosophical 'heterodoxy'[1]—communicates itself to the reader on
every page.

Genesis of the Text

The impression Nietzsche gives in *Ecce Homo* of having produced
Twilight from scratch in a matter of days is a little misleading. The
composition of the first draft did indeed take place at a furious pace,
and on the day he sent the manuscript to his publisher, 9 September, he
wrote to his friend Carl Fuchs describing how in recent weeks he had
felt 'most uncommonly *inspired*': 'I would quite often get up (or rather
jump up) at two in the morning, "driven by the spirit" to dash something off' (KGB III/5, 414). But the main reason it took shape so
quickly was that he was able to use a good deal of material which he had
already collected together with a different purpose in mind, for the
book emerged as the result of an important change of tack which
Nietzsche's publication plans underwent during the summer of
1888. Despite the fact that since the early 1870s he had been publishing
more or less a new book per year, since 1885 he had also been amassing a
large stock of notes and drafts in preparation for launching on the
world what was to have been his *magnum opus*, *The Will to Power*. He
had already raided these notes for *Beyond Good and Evil* (1886) and *On
the Genealogy of Morals* (1887), and in the summer of 1888 he finally
abandoned the project of *The Will to Power* altogether, deciding to
recast the remaining material as a new four-part masterwork to be
called 'Revaluation of All Values' ('Umwerthung aller Werthe'). This
breakthrough allowed him to overcome a rare period of writer's block
(as late as 22 August he was writing to his friend Meta von Salis that he
feared the whole summer had been a 'washout'—KGB III/5, 397), and
it was at this point that his work on *Twilight* began—as a release, a
distraction, or in the medical terms of Nietzsche's own later Foreword,
a 'recuperation', a 'convalescence'. But Nietzsche's mood in such a
period of spiritual convalescence is very far removed from the sublime
and tranquil piety of Beethoven's Op. 132 quartet, with its 'Convalescent's Hymn of Thanksgiving to the Divinity'. In the Preface to the

---

[1] Cf. Nietzsche's letters to Paul Deussen, 14 Sept. 1888, and Franz Overbeck, 18 Oct.
1888, in *Selected Letters of Friedrich Nietzsche*, ed. and trans. Christopher Middleton
(Chicago and London: University of Chicago Press, 1969), 311 and 315. Cf. also KGB
III/5, 417, 434 and Sarah Kofman, *Explosion II: Les Enfants de Nietzsche* (Paris: Galilée,
1993), 307–16 ('Hétérodoxie').

second edition of *The Gay Science* (1887), Nietzsche refers instead to 'the *intoxication* of convalescence' (GS, 'Preface' 1): for him, convalescence is a *riot*, a 'Saturnalia of the spirit', to be celebrated with all the renewed Dionysian strength at one's disposal, impishly and impiously.

Nietzsche's Styles

It comes as no surprise, then, that the first thing Nietzsche himself should remark on when discussing *Twilight*, both in *Ecce Homo* and in the Foreword to the work itself, is its tone: 'fateful' because of the enormity of the task still to be completed (the 'gloomy and exceedingly responsible business' which is the 'Revaluation'), but leavened with levity, 'cheerful', 'sunny', and 'high-spirited'. In this respect alone Nietzsche distinguishes himself in *Twilight* from the tradition of German academic philosophy against which he is writing. Immanuel Kant, to take one of his favourite counter-examples, concedes in a letter to Moses Mendelssohn concerning his *Critique of Pure Reason* (1781): 'I completed it hastily . . ., with the greatest attentiveness to its content but less care about its style and ease of comprehension.'[2] In *Twilight*, on the contrary, Nietzsche shows himself to be a master of stylistic virtuosity, and the speed of its execution is merely a symptom of his assuredness in this regard: of all his texts it is perhaps the best vindication of his claim (in *Ecce Homo*) to have 'the most manifold art of style any man has ever had at his disposal' (EH III 4). In accordance with his standard practice it is divided into numbered paragraphs, but in Nietzsche's hands the paragraph becomes an extraordinarily supple unit which can vary in length from a single line to a full three pages.

Nietzsche is also keen to achieve 'ease of comprehension' here, as one might expect of a text which was intended, on one level at least, to be a kind of primer in his philosophy. This had not always been the case, however, for he was more used to playing a game of cat and mouse with his readers: his ambivalence over whether he actually even wanted to be read and understood is summed up by the defiant subtitle to *Thus Spake Zarathustra* (1883–5), 'A Book for Everyone and No One', and in *Beyond Good and Evil* he states quite openly that 'I am doing everything I can to make myself "hard to understand"' (BGE 27). Yet in the works of 1888—by which stage he knew he was

---

[2] *Kant: Philosophical Correspondence, 1759–99*, ed. and trans. Arnulf Zweig (Chicago and London: University of Chicago Press, 1967), 105 f.

reaching a wider readership at last, since the influential Danish philosopher Georg Brandes had begun to lecture on him in Copenhagen—he becomes much more accommodating, to the point where 'Have I been understood?' punctuates the last paragraphs of *Ecce Homo* like a refrain (EH IV 7–9). In *Twilight*, too, Nietzsche clearly has a 'mission to explain': to bring out his key points he makes very frequent use of emphasis (rendered here by italics); he gives copious illustrative examples (e.g. VI 1; VII 2; IX 22) and is happy to condense 'an essential new insight into four theses' by way of 'easing comprehension' (III 6), indeed to sloganize and present memorable 'formulas' (I 44; V 4; VII 5). He devotes entire paragraphs to clarifying what he means by 'My Idea of Freedom' (IX 38), 'My Idea of Genius' (IX 44), or 'Progress in My Sense' (IX 48), while elsewhere the text gives the appearance of a catechism, as questions like 'What can *our* doctrine be, though?' (VI 8) are duly answered.

Despite these didactic features, *Twilight* still does not always make things easy for its readers: the exuberance and inventiveness of Nietzsche's philosophical mind are matched by a penchant for puns, parodies, neologisms, and other linguistic play. He jokes that his stylistic deftness will make him 'a complete riddle to German readers' (VIII 7), but he is still writing in the first instance for readers of German, so it is all the more unavoidable that a translator will need at times to append glosses in order to give readers the full flavour of his prose. For good measure, he is never averse to peppering his German with words and phrases from some of the other languages at his disposal—primarily French and Latin, but occasionally English, Spanish, or ancient Greek. He is writing for an educated, cosmopolitan nineteenth-century readership and naturally presupposes a knowledge of the classical and major modern European languages, but he presupposes a good deal else besides, for his range of reference and allusion in *Twilight* is immense—not 'just' the whole Western tradition in philosophy and religion, but Indian and Chinese thinkers too, classical and modern literature, history, historiography, and political theory, as well as contemporary developments across the natural sciences. As far as his own previous works are concerned, he generally (though not invariably) provides references to allow his readers to check back to them when necessary, but given their dismal sales figures this would seem more a hope than an expectation, and in any case he specializes in quoting himself out of context.

Yet in one sense Nietzsche remains the most accessible of philosophers, for his style is mercifully jargon-free—and he mercilessly sends up the technical terms coined by his philosophical predecessors, such as Leibniz's 'principle of sufficient reason' (VIII 4) or Kant's 'thing in itself' (VI 3). Nietzsche is an 'ordinary language' philosopher *avant la lettre*, and it is ironic that his work was shunned by those in the 'analytic' tradition of philosophy who rallied under that banner. Willy-nilly, certain of his usages do inevitably assume the status of technical terms and acquire a density as they recur from one work to the next, but they are relatively few, for in stark contrast to Kant and his philosophical progeny Nietzsche does not consider the erection of monumental conceptual structures to be a proof of philosophical manhood. In fact, quite the opposite: 'I mistrust all systematists and avoid them. The will to system is a lack of integrity' (I 26). That is not to say that his writings will therefore amount to no more than a jumble of disconnected thoughts, as some less sympathetic commentators have supposed: systematicity and coherence are two different things. Much of Nietzsche's notebook material was jotted down while he was away from his desk, avoiding the danger of 'conceptual cobwebbery' (IX 23)—we can take him literally when he writes in the Foreword of 'run[ning] out into the sunshine', and in any case he tells us explicitly that '[o]nly thoughts which come from *walking* have any value' (I 34)—but what he does not mention is the effort which he then put into the compilation and redaction of the fragmentary material which inevitably resulted. Even the most loosely organized of *Twilight*'s sections, 'Maxims and Barbs', is not so much unsystematic as studiedly *anti*-systematic: the placement of the remark on philosophical systematists quoted above is instructive, for it disrupts a short sequence of aphorisms on woman (I 25, 27–8) which might otherwise have formed a thematic unit. But 'Maxims and Barbs' is an exception in the context of the work as a whole, for although it is true that *Twilight* is not 'through-composed' in the sense that, say, *The Birth of Tragedy* (1872) or *On the Genealogy of Morals* are—Nietzsche's range of subjects here is much wider—it is perhaps surprising, given the contingencies of the text's production, that the sections should exhibit quite such a degree of individual integrity and collective interconnection.

Topsy-Turvy Truths

On the technical level, then, *Twilight of the Idols* is a highly sophisticated rhetorical accomplishment, but the effervescent tonic is laced with vitriol, for it is also a masterpiece of polemic: as Nietzsche puts it in the Foreword, 'this little work is a *great declaration of war*'. In this sense it continues in the spirit of its immediate predecessors *On the Genealogy of Morals*—explicitly subtitled 'A Polemic'—and the work which Nietzsche was still seeing to press at the time of *Twilight*'s composition, *The Wagner Case*, a *casus belli* which he referred to in private as 'my "declaration of war" against Wagner'.[3] It is clear from Nietzsche's correspondence that *Twilight* was intended as a companion piece to *The Wagner Case*—he insisted to his publisher, for example, that its presentation should be identical to that of its 'twin' (KGB III/5, 412)—but only in the sense that, having settled his score with Wagner, he would draw the line under some of his numerous other quarrels. For although the title, a parody of Wagner's *Twilight of the Gods*, might lead one to expect another tirade against the former mentor whose histrionic aesthetic and Christianized, nationalistic ideology he now found repugnant, Nietzsche had already spent his anti-Wagnerian ammunition in the previous text (the late *Nietzsche contra Wagner* is a collection of slightly modified excerpts from his pre-1888 works), and references to Wagner in *Twilight* itself are very sparse indeed.[4]

Instead, Nietzsche in *Twilight* is much more wide-ranging in his approach. His aim, as Walter Kaufmann and Gilles Deleuze rightly point out, is nothing less than to out-Kant Kant and mount a thoroughgoing critique of all philosophical values hitherto.[5] His targets are what he considers to be all the unexamined prejudices

---

[3] Letter to Paul Deussen, 14 Sept. 1888, in *Selected Letters*, 310; cf. also KGB III/5, 434, 440, 447.

[4] Cf. VIII 4; IX 4, 30. Nietzsche excised a further reference to Wagner which had been present in his notes (KGW VIII/3, 272); his letter to Heinrich Köselitz of 27 Sept. 1888 (KGB III/5, 443) makes it clear that he considered the title's Wagnerian echo to be of only secondary importance, and this is confirmed by his letters to potential French and English translators of the work (KGB III/5, 535, 537), where he suggests they adopt the alternative title 'Hammer of the Idols' (*Götzen-Hammer/Marteau des Idoles*), thus dropping the Wagnerian reference altogether.

[5] Cf. Walter Kaufmann, *Nietzsche: Philosopher, Psychologist, Antichrist*, 4th edn. (Princeton: Princeton University Press, 1974), 114, and Gilles Deleuze, *Nietzsche and Philosophy*, trans. Hugh Tomlinson (London: Athlone Press; New York: Columbia University Press, 1983), 1.

which have been masquerading as truths for millennia and wor-
shipped as such by the uncomprehending 'populace', philosophical
and non-philosophical alike, such as 'that Socratic equation, reason = virtue = happiness' (II 4). His method is in the strictest sense
revolutionary, for it consists in debasing the highest values and
toppling them from their pedestals, inverting the established hier-
archies as a prelude to their deconstruction, and it is ironic—given
that Nietzsche never read Marx—that in describing this procedure
he should reach for the same metaphor of righting everything which
was 'topsy-turvy' which Marx used in describing his own relation to
Hegel.[6] In *Twilight*, Nietzsche brings to a culmination the project
which he had announced a decade earlier in the programmatic first
paragraph of *Human, All Too Human*, that of unmasking the mun-
dane origins of seemingly transcendent goods, subjecting them to a
'genealogical' reduction in order to reveal that 'the most glorious
colours are derived from base, indeed from despised materials' (HA
I 1), reducing the grand explanatory gestures of idealist metaphysics
to the level of 'little unpretentious truths' (HA I 3).[7] But *Twilight*
looks forwards as well as backwards—Peter Pütz reminds us that the
very term 'twilight' is ambiguous (in English as in German) since it
can connote both evening and morning[8]—so that when Nietzsche
describes the book in *Ecce Homo* as an act of 'subversion' or 'over-
throwing' ('Umwerfung'), this term also anticipates the project of
revaluation ('Umwerthung') to which it was intended as a prelude.

In *Twilight* Nietzsche presents himself as an iconoclast, a destroyer
of idols, for which task he equips himself with the hammer of the

[6] Cf. Marx's 1872 Preface to *Capital*, vol. I: 'With him, [the dialectic] is standing on its
head. It must be turned right side up again' (*Karl Marx: Selected Writings*, ed. David
McLellan (Oxford: Oxford University Press, 1977), 420). For the trope of inversion in
Marx, Freud, and Nietzsche, cf. Sarah Kofman, *Camera obscura: de l'idéologie* (Paris:
Galilée, 1973).

[7] In his Introduction to *Human, All Too Human* (Cambridge: Cambridge University
Press, 1986), Erich Heller comments: 'Most of the psychological "unmasking" in
Nietzsche's works after *Human, All Too Human* is brilliantly performed with instruments
constructed for that book' (p. xiii). Nietzsche himself was keen to underline the con-
tinuities between this work and later ones, as in the Preface to *On the Genealogy of Morals*
(GM, 'Preface' 2 and 4) or, in *Twilight*, at IX 39, where he includes a quotation from
Human, All Too Human which he had had to have specially supplied by his friend Franz
Overbeck (cf. KGB III/5, 449), since he did not take copies of his own works with him on
his travels.

[8] Cf. Peter Pütz, 'Nachwort' to Friedrich Nietzsche, *Der Fall Wagner, Götzen-
Dämmerung, Nietzsche contra Wagner*, ed. Peter Pütz (Munich: Goldmann, 1988), 184.

book's subtitle—a veritable Swiss army hammer which tolls the
death knell for philosophy as it has traditionally been understood
and has the final word in the text when it speaks in section XI,
boasting its hardness. There are still more aspects to this multi-
purpose implement, though, for in the Foreword Nietzsche develops
the metaphor further, writing that 'it is not contemporary idols but
eternal idols that are being touched here with a hammer as if with a
tuning fork'. Here the musical and the medical are conflated in a
much more delicate operation, with Nietzsche adopting the guise of
'The Philosopher as Cultural Physician',[9] wielding his hammer as a
diagnostic tool in order to 'sound out' all the hollow idols by a process
of auscult(ur)ation. Despite his contention, though, it is undoubtedly
both 'eternal' and 'contemporary idols' that come under Nietzsche's
diagnostic hammer in this text: on the one hand those 'truths' which
have passed for such since the dawn of Western philosophy in ancient
Greece, such as 'The Four Great Errors' of section VI, on the other
the ills of contemporary European culture such as statism, the worship of that 'new idol' which he had already warned against in *Thus
Spake Zarathustra* (Z I; cf. GS 24). In *Ecce Homo* Nietzsche describes
another earlier text, *Beyond Good and Evil*, as 'in all essentials a
critique of modernity' (EH III 'BGE' 2), but 'Critique of Modernity'
is the very title he uses for one of the paragraphs in *Twilight* (IX 39):
he adopts the position of 'untimely man' here (IX) precisely in order
to get a hermeneutic handle on those 'signs of the times' whose
significance would otherwise be overlooked. As he explains to his
friend Franz Overbeck in a letter discussing the text: 'it is very
"timely": I pay my "compliments" to all possible thinkers and artists
in today's Europe.'[10]

Health of Nations

The two nationalities which Dr Nietzsche singles out for particular
treatment 'in today's Europe' are the two which had always most
absorbed him: the Germans and the French. As far as the Germans

[9] A title Nietzsche considered for the early unpublished work 'Philosophy in the
Tragic Age of the Greeks' (1873). Cf. Daniel R. Ahern, *Nietzsche as Cultural Physician*
(University Park, Pa.: Pennsylvania State University Press, 1995).
[10] Letter to Franz Overbeck, 14 Sept. 1888 (KGB III/5, 434). On the importance of
the term 'untimely' to Nietzsche, cf. my article 'On "Untimeliness": Temporal Structures in Nietzsche; or, "The Day After Tomorrow Belongs to Me"', *Journal of Nietzsche
Studies*, 8 (Autumn 1994), 33–53.

are concerned, Nietzsche certainly held no special brief for the country of his birth: from as early as 1873 and the first of his *Untimely Meditations, David Strauss the Confessor and the Writer*, he had mercilessly attacked the cultural wilderness which was Germany in the Bismarck era as he saw it. He never went so far as to publish a *Nietzsche contra Deutschland* (for one thing he had a justifiable fear of censorship), but this attitude is implicit in all but his earliest writings, and it intensifies over his philosophical career so that by 1888 he had even managed to convince himself (erroneously, as it turns out) that he was of ancient Polish stock, and the very last piece he composed was a declaration of 'Deadly War against the House of Hohenzollern' (KGW VIII/3, 457–61). The material which he did choose to publish as section VIII of *Twilight*, entitled 'What the Germans Lack', could scarcely be more explicit on this count, and indeed Nietzsche considered the book's anti-German slant to be one of its main selling-points abroad, as he explained in a letter to a prospective English translator, at the same time judiciously omitting to mention the book's no less explicit criticisms of 'the English fatheads' (IX 5), this 'nation of complete cant' (IX 12).[11]

Nietzsche's attitude towards French culture is a very different matter, though, for he had been holding up the French as an 'antidote' to the Germans ever since 1871, the year in which Germany united and the Reich was founded in the wake of the Franco-Prussian War. He had familiarized himself with French classical drama as early as the late 1860s, when working on his first book, *The Birth of Tragedy*, and in the mid-1870s he had devoted a good deal of time to the writings of French philosophers such as Montaigne, Pascal, La Rochefoucauld, Rousseau, and Voltaire (to whom he dedicated the first edition of *Human, All Too Human*). He pays homage to these writers in *Ecce Homo* when he remarks: 'It is really only a small number of older Frenchmen to whom I return again and again: I believe only in French culture and consider everything in Europe that calls itself "culture" a misunderstanding, not to speak of German culture...' (EH II 3). But by the 1880s he had become increasingly fascinated with the French culture of his own century, and not so much with France's philosophers, for whom he had scant respect, as with French literary writers (Stendhal, Baudelaire, Flaubert,

George Sand), historians (Ernest Renan, Hippolyte Taine), and above all, psychologists. As he writes in *Twilight*:

At the same moment as Germany is rising up as a great power, France is gaining a new importance as a *cultural power*. By now a great deal of new intellectual seriousness and *passion* has already moved over to Paris: the question of pessimism, for example, the question of Wagner, practically all psychological and artistic questions are given incomparably more sensitive and thorough consideration there than in Germany. (VIII 4; cf. EH II 4)

This is not to say that Nietzsche saw France as somehow untainted by the cultural malaise which he diagnosed elsewhere in Europe—indeed quite the opposite, for the enthusiasm with which Paris had embraced Wagnerism provided him with an object lesson in the creeping corruption of cultural 'health'. What made contemporary French culture different for Nietzsche was the way in which French psychological writers had developed the means with which to analyse and critique their own cultural decline, and Nietzsche in turn paid tribute to the acumen of these writers in his writings of 1888, not merely through such overt flattery as in the passage above, but also more implicitly and effectively through borrowing their terms of analysis. Thus many of *Twilight*'s more acerbic comments on French writers, in sections I and IX in particular, can be traced back to the *Journal* of the brothers Goncourt, from which Nietzsche excerpted copiously in his notebooks, and his whole conception of 'decadence' would be inconceivable without the 'Theory of Decadence' which he borrowed from the section on Baudelaire in Paul Bourget's *Essays in Contemporary Psychology* (1883).[12] An important indicator of Nietzsche's debt to Bourget is the fact that he uses the French word *décadence* throughout both *The Wagner Case* and *Twilight* because no German word for it had yet been coined; a similar case is the conspicuously neologistic loan-word 'Degenerescenz', which makes a number of appearances in *Twilight* after Nietzsche avidly read Charles Féré's recently published *Degenerescence and Criminality* in the spring of 1888.[13] Such examples throw a new light on

[12] Cf. Mazzino Montinari, 'Aufgaben der Nietzsche-Forschung heute: Nietzsches Auseinandersetzung mit der französischen Literatur des 19. Jahrhunderts', in *Nietzsche heute. Die Rezeption seines Werkes nach 1968*, ed. Sigrid Bauschinger, Susan L. Cocalis, and Sara Lennox (Bern and Stuttgart: Francke, 1988), 143–6.

[13] Cf. Mazzino Montinari, 'Nietzsche lesen: Die Götzen-Dämmerung', *Nietzsche-Studien*, 13 (1984), 76.

Nietzsche's remark in a letter of 12 September 1888 to his friend and amanuensis Heinrich Köselitz (Peter Gast): 'between ourselves, it strikes me that it is only this year that I have learnt to write German—I mean *French*' (KGB III/5, 417).[14]

'Idleness of a Psychologist'

So Nietzsche's reading of these contemporary French psychological writers had a profound impact on him which is traceable to the very terms of his philosophical analysis, and for all his attempts to present *Twilight* as a synopsis of his philosophy as a whole, to emphasize its continuities with his earlier works, the fact remains that along with the other works of 1888 it bristles with a register of vocabulary which is decidedly new in Nietzsche's works, a vocabulary derived from psychology and physiology, from pathology, symptomatology ('semiotics' in the strict sense), and medicine. 'For a psychologist there are few questions that are as attractive as that concerning the relation of health and philosophy', Nietzsche writes in the Preface to the second edition of *The Gay Science* (GS, 'Preface' 2), but it is in the works of 1888, and *Twilight* in particular, that Nietzsche the cultural physician finally dons his surgical mask in earnest (jocularity) and enters the operating theatre. 'A peculiar hospital air wafts towards us from many pages of *Twilight of the Idols*', comments Mazzino Montinari, co-editor of the standard German edition of Nietzsche's works;[15] in *Ecce Homo*, Nietzsche himself adopts a more self-congratulatory tone in speaking of what he terms his 'medi-cynicism': 'That out of my writings there speaks a *psychologist* who has not his equal, that is perhaps the first thing a good reader will notice' (EH III 5).

In this context it should be noted that Nietzsche originally gave *Twilight of the Idols* a very different working title, 'Idleness of a Psychologist' ('Müssiggang eines Psychologen'), and although he

---

[14] It is significant that in seeking to have *Twilight* translated, Nietzsche's best efforts were directed towards securing a French translator for it, and the same applied to *Ecce Homo*, for which his first choice of French publisher was Bourget's publisher Lemerre. Cf. letter to August Strindberg, 8 Dec. 1888, in *Selected Letters* (incorrectly dated 7 Dec.), 330.

[15] 'Nietzsche lesen', 76. Michel Serres describes *The Antichrist* in similar terms as 'a handbook of medicine', 'a vade mecum of microbiology' ('Corruption—*The Antichrist*: A Chemistry of Sensations and Ideas', trans. Chris Bongie, in *Nietzsche in Italy*, ed. Thomas Harrison (Saratoga, Calif.: ANMA Libri, 1988), 32).

eventually abandoned this title in late September 1888 at the prompt-
ing of Köselitz, who sycophantically urged him to substitute something altogether more grandiose (cf. KGB III/6, 309 f.), nevertheless
traces of it survive in the published text, in the Foreword and the very
first aphorism in 'Maxims and Barbs'. The etymology of 'Müssiggang'—'leisurely stroll'—underlines the intimate relation between
thinking and walking which Nietzsche wants to establish, and the
low-key, unpretentious resonances of this projected title tell us a
good deal about the text as a whole, for *Twilight* is largely free of the
declamatory heroics and overweening sense of self-importance which
would surface so soon, and so spectacularly, in *Ecce Homo*. Despite
the fact that much of the text was initially intended for *The Will to
Power*, what is perhaps surprising is that Nietzsche the philosopher of
power is largely absent here, and that the 'grand doctrines' which he
had been working out predominantly in his notebooks of the later
1880s with *The Will to Power* in mind—'nihilism', 'perspectivism',
'will to power' itself—are very much in abeyance. Instead, as in *The
Gay Science* (GS 329), he places a premium on 'idleness' or 'leisure', a
virtue with a long pedigree stretching back to Aristotle and Cicero,
and one which finds its most eloquent twentieth-century advocate in
that unlikeliest of Nietzscheans, Bertrand Russell.[16] (It might seem
strange to the English-speaking reader that Nietzsche, that most
inveterate of punsters, should have failed to exploit the obvious
pun on 'idol'/'idle', but it was not available to him in German, and
although he certainly had enough English to pun on 'Kant'/'cant'
(IX 1), his command of the language was not extensive.)

The very title of the text, then, was a late change made at the proof
stage, and this is typical of the text as a whole, whose composition was
altered at a number of points on the way to the final version, through
additions and accretions, revisions and excisions. The main reason
for this was that in the September and October of 1888 Nietzsche was
working simultaneously on three texts (*Twilight*, *The Antichrist*, and,
from 15 October, *Ecce Homo*), and constantly facing decisions about
what to include in which, generating new material all the while. Thus
the first draft of *Twilight* actually included what would become the

---

[16] Cf. Bertrand Russell, 'In Praise of Idleness', in *In Praise of Idleness and Other Essays*
(London: Unwin, 1976), 11–25. Elsewhere, Russell makes his distaste for Nietzsche's
philosophy patent—cf. *History of Western Philosophy*, 2nd edn. (London: George Allen
and Unwin, 1961), 728–39.

first twenty-four paragraphs of *The Antichrist*,[17] but in the weeks following completion of that draft the rest of *The Antichrist* took shape, so that on 30 September 1888 the divorce between the two texts was sealed when Nietzsche finished *Twilight* with the dated Foreword. As a consequence, though, this Foreword bears the peculiar distinction of announcing the completion of a different text from the one it precedes, 'the first book of the *Revaluation of all Values*', i.e. *The Antichrist*.

In the Foreword itself, as we have seen, Nietzsche sounds some of the main themes for the work to come, but stylistically the Foreword also provides us with a paradigmatic introduction to his use of metaphor. The first sentence sets up an opposition between 'gloomy' and 'cheerful' which quite naturally opens out into a broader metaphorics of darkness and light (the black question mark, the shadow, sunshine), since the German words 'düster' and 'heiter' can refer interchangeably to a person's mood and to atmospheric conditions. The first part of the Foreword thus elaborates what one might call an extended 'light-motif', exploiting a 'heliotropic' semantic field which on the one hand, of course, is that of the title, but which also links *Twilight* to others of Nietzsche's works dating as far back as *Daybreak* (1881) and, once more, *Human, All Too Human* (HA I 107).[18] After the interpolated Latin quotation, however, the Foreword changes tack, and with the play on 'evil eye' and 'evil ear' the predominantly visual metaphors modulate into auditory ones (the 'sounding out' of idols, Nietzsche as 'Pied Piper'), so that as well as 'illustrating' the metaphorical potential of the title, the passage also 'echoes' that of the subtitle, the hammer-as-tuning-fork.[19]

Survey of the Sections

It is appropriate that the first section of the book, 'Maxims and Barbs', should be aphoristic in character, for not only had writers

---

[17] Cf. Montinari, 'Nietzsche lesen', 74. The intimate relation between the two texts is confirmed by *Ecce Homo*, where Nietzsche's comments on *The Antichrist* in 'Why I Write Such Good Books' are included in the section ostensibly devoted to *Twilight* alone.

[18] Cf. Bernard Pautrat, *Versions du soleil: Figures et système de Nietzsche* (Paris: Seuil, 1971), and Sarah Kofman, *Nietzsche and Metaphor*, trans. Duncan Large (London: Athlone Press; Stanford: Stanford University Press, 1993), 110 f.

[19] For further thoughts on 'the circular complicity of the metaphors of the eye and the ear', cf. Jacques Derrida, 'Tympan', in *Margins of Philosophy*, trans. Alan Bass (Chicago: University of Chicago Press; Hassocks: Harvester, 1982), pp. ix–xxix.

such as Lichtenberg and the French *moralistes*, with whom Nietzsche was intimately familiar, established the aphorism as the vehicle *par excellence* for acute psychological observation, but the principle which forms the basis of Nietzsche's method in *Twilight*, the inversion of received wisdoms, lends itself ideally to stylistic expression in this form.[20] A collection of aphorisms like this is a typical feature of Nietzsche's earlier books (for example, the 'Assorted Opinions and Maxims' of *Human, All Too Human*, Book II (1879), Book III of *The Gay Science* (1882), or the 'Maxims and Interludes' which make up Part 4 of *Beyond Good and Evil*), and indeed 'Maxims and Barbs' itself grew out of the 'Maxims of a Hyperborean' which he collected together in the spring of 1888 from earlier notebooks (KGW VIII/3, 271–4), in some cases dating back as far as 1881.[21] However, this is the first and only occasion on which Nietzsche begins a book with such a series, thus pointing up its polemical, combative character.

'Nothing succeeds without high spirits playing their part', we are told in the Foreword, and the first section is particularly playful, with Nietzsche often taking a proverb, homily, or otherwise 'time-honoured truth'—such as 'The Devil finds work for idle hands to do' in the very first paragraph (I 1), 'All truth is simple' (I 4), or 'He who laughs last, laughs longest' (I 43)—and displacing it slightly, giving it a new twist, or completely inverting it, so as to debunk it and make us question its validity. Such saws are precisely the kind of fraudulent 'eternal idols' Nietzsche is out to unseat: at the beginning of the next section (II 1) he will explicitly take issue with the 'consensus of the wise'; here he is already squaring up to 'the wisest of all ages' more implicitly, by disputing the claim of even the cosiest, most consensual 'truths' to universalizability. In the first section Nietzsche also directs his dissent at more localized targets, though—he gives us 'barbs' as well as (subverted) 'maxims'—and just as he will insist that all proverbial sayings have a provenance (even if a relatively vague one, a conspiracy among 'the wisest of all ages'), so he typically attacks not a belief, opinion, or doctrine but its exponents. He introduces us in this section to a heterogeneous *population* of 'idolaters', cowards, and hypocrites, ranging from groups such as anti-Semites (I 19) and nihilists (I 34), historians (I 24) and philosophical systematists (I 26), to whole nationalities in the cases of the English

---

[20] Cf. Pütz, 185–9.   [21] Cf. Montinari, 'Nietzsche lesen', 70.

(I 12), the Russians (I 22), and the Germans (I 23): in spite of his assaults on the pettiness of nationalistic sentiment (IX 39) he is not averse to using national stereotypes as shorthand. Nothing is sacred, nothing taboo, for when Nietzsche is on the offensive he does not shy away from giving offence, and a number of his remarks on woman, in particular (I 25, 27, 28), make uncomfortable reading.

This technique of personalizing the cut and thrust of philosophical argument has important implications, both methodological and stylistic. On the one hand we can immediately sense that for Nietzsche every philosophical principle needs to be approached as an expression (a 'symptom') of the psycho-physiology of the individual who holds it: philosophical positions, and moral codes in particular, are not abstract 'eternal verities' (HA I 11) but the products of historical circumstances and configurations of forces, so traditional philosophical analysis must be superseded by a new practice of philosophy as symptomatology, a historical taxonomy or 'genealogy' of human types. On the other hand, by conjuring up an array of antagonists Nietzsche animates his philosophical style and turns differences of opinion into dramatized vignettes acted out between a whole cast of characters, a plurality of voices among which the philosophical 'I' is but one (and not the most frequent, either). The commonest pronoun in 'Maxims and Barbs' is in fact the German 'man'—the (ungendered) impersonal voice of the generality, the 'herd', the 'people' who 'say'[22]—but the variety of voices Nietzsche orchestrates in this opening section alone is astonishing, and he runs the whole grammatical gamut from the first person singular to the third person plural, the majority of paragraphs being (at least implicitly) polyphonic, conversational.

And it is a conversation in which the reader is expressly invited to participate, whether she or he is being buttonholed by the text's explicit interpellations in the second person singular, as in the series of 'questions for the conscience' with which the section draws to a close, or more indirectly addressed by Nietzsche's rhetorical questions. Indeed, despite the fact that this opening section is entitled 'Maxims and Barbs', the commonest form among these short paragraphs is that of the question—there are thirty-nine question marks

[22] This is the same pronoun Heidegger will substantivize as 'the They' in section 27 of *Being and Time*.

in all, or almost one per paragraph. Nor is this the only punctuational means by which Nietzsche invites the reader to join in the debate (more precisely, to agree with him): one of the most distinctive features of his style is the welter of dashes and dots with which he so often chooses to 'link' sentences. For all the forcefulness of his articulation (and exclamation marks also abound), his paragraphs themselves are but weakly articulated, by means of 'Gedanken-striche' (thought dashes) which call on the reader's thoughts to bridge the gaps, and ellipses or aposiopeses where Nietzsche breaks off and leaves it to the reader to complete the sense, *challenging* the reader to respond and add his or her voice. In each case it is as though Nietzsche were signalling to the reader in a kind of parodic Morse code: 'over to you'.

Nietzsche cultivates non-closure in these ways throughout the work; moreover, this paratactic, elliptical style can be observed on a larger scale in the links between paragraphs and sections as well. By far the majority of all the paragraphs in *Twilight* end inconclusively on an ellipsis, a dash, or a question mark—in sections III, V, and X *every* paragraph does. Similarly, every section (including the last) ends openly in one of these ways, with the single exception of section IV, which might just as well have done since it ends with a begin-ning ('INCIPIT ZARATHUSTRA'). Recent Nietzsche-inspired post-structuralist commentators have stressed the openness of any text to potentially infinite interpretation, its deflection on to the reader of the responsibility for constituting meaning out of its 'dissemination',[23] but one need not go as far as Deleuze—'An aphorism means nothing, signifies nothing'[24]—to note the extraordinary openness in the weave of Nietzsche's philosophical texture which he achieves through such devices as these.

The formal contrast between the first and second sections in *Twi-light* is the sharpest in the book, engineered for maximum effect: the pithy pyrotechnics of 'Maxims and Barbs' give way to 'The Problem

[23] Cf. Jacques Derrida, *Dissemination*, trans. Barbara Johnson (Chicago: University of Chicago Press; London: Athlone Press, 1981). For the application of this approach to Nietzsche, cf. Derrida, *Spurs: Nietzsche's Styles/ Éperons: Les Styles de Nietzsche*, trans. Barbara Harlow (Chicago and London: University of Chicago Press, 1979), and Kofman, *Nietzsche and Metaphor*, 114–18.

[24] Gilles Deleuze, 'Nomad Thought', trans. David B. Allison, in *The New Nietzsche: Contemporary Styles of Interpretation*, 2nd edn., ed. David B. Allison (Cambridge, Mass.: MIT Press, 1985), 145.

of Socrates', a series of linked reflections which amount to one long
case history of Socrates and his decadent *milieu* similar in execution
to *The Wagner Case*. Nietzsche here passes from generalized, impersonal statements of 'wisdom' to his archetypal representative of 'the
wisest of all ages': he gives us his last word on the philosopher who
has been one of his prime sparring partners since *The Birth of
Tragedy*,[25] except that he now sees Socrates no longer as the *instigator*
of Greek decadence, as in the earlier text, but rather as its *expression*.
In 'The Four Great Errors' Nietzsche will repeatedly warn against
confusing cause and consequence (VI 1); here, in keeping with his
own injunction, he discreetly revises his earlier judgement of the
philosopher—though this does not prevent him citing *The Birth of
Tragedy* (II 2) as though his reflections here were merely a continua-
tion in the same vein. We need to beware of such surreptitious
retrospective modifications, which are typical of Nietzsche's late
writings—he will do the same again at IX 10, a striking revision of
the view he had put forward in *The Birth of Tragedy* of the relation
between the 'Apollonian' and the 'Dionysian' which is nevertheless
presented as a synopsis of it. 'Remorse is indecent', he tells us (I 10),
and he himself lives up to this maxim by refusing to turn his back on
his own earlier works—even the very earliest, from which he has
departed the furthest—but this deceptive 'continuity' is achieved
only by dint of such undeclared adjustments. In this respect *Twilight*
shares the same project as *Ecce Homo* and *Nietzsche contra Wagner*: it
is a recuperation, not just in the medical sense of its Foreword but
also in the sense that in it Nietzsche recuperates or rehabilitates his
earlier philosophical positions by subtly reinterpreting them.

Nietzsche's analysis of Socrates in 'The Problem of Socrates' also
differs from that of *The Birth of Tragedy* because—to use his own
striking analogy (VI 6)—he has 'translated' it into a new 'dialect', that
of his new diagnostic disciplines, symptomatology (II 2) and pathology (II 10). The term 'idiosyncrasy' (II 4, 9) plays a key role here,
for Nietzsche exploits the original sense of the term ('physical
constitution peculiar to a person') in order to trace the Socratic
revolution in 'taste' and 'manners' (the rise of dialectics) back to
such physiological factors as 'instinctual anarchy', a 'superfetation of

---

[25] For the history of Nietzsche's figurations of Socrates, cf. Sarah Kofman, *Socrate(s)*
(Paris: Galilée, 1990).

the logical', 'jaundiced malice', 'auditory hallucinations' (II 4), and so on. Socrates emerges as such a monstrous caricature—not so much a case as a head case—that one is tempted to accuse Nietzsche himself of 'jaundiced malice', yet there are more than just hints here of a sneaking admiration for his (in)famous forebear (a hammer, after all, is not a hatchet). Not only was Socrates apparently cunning enough to hoodwink an entire culture (II 6), he was able to do so because he had a supreme psychological understanding of the extent and nature of the crisis which that culture was then facing, and because he had already succeeded in overcoming his own decadent desires, in becoming master of himself (II 9). There are thus surprising similarities between the portrait of Socrates Nietzsche gives us here and that of Goethe later on in the text—a figure who also 'disciplined himself into a whole' (IX 49), whom Nietzsche himself was most tempted to idolize—or indeed Nietzsche's parodic *self*-portraits in *Ecce Homo*, as satyr (EH, 'Preface' 2), *décadent* (EH I 2), buffoon (EH IV 1).[26] For Nietzsche, Socrates' problematic 'case' is the most interesting in the history of philosophy because he stands on the threshold between the 'festive' philosophy of figures such as Heraclitus (III 2)—'Philosophy in the Tragic Age of the Greeks'—and the dark age of the 'tyranny of reason' which he himself inaugurates: he intrudes on the philosophical feast like a crepuscular *Commendatore*, dragging philosophy—indeed European culture as a whole—down into a netherworld from which, through Nietzsche's own writings, it has only recently re-emerged (cf. IV).

Where Freud picks on *Oedipus Tyrannus* as the archetype for his drama of psychosexual development, Nietzsche here constructs his own classical tyrant figure to play an equivalent role in his narrative of the fate of philosophy. In the next section, ' "Reason" in Philosophy', he pans out again from the idiosyncrasy of one particular philosopher to the idiosyncrasies (III 1, 4) of philosophers as a class, but because the whole Western tradition in philosophy has fallen under the sway of the 'tyranny of reason' Nietzsche derives the same diagnosis as before: it is 'decadent' (III 6), afflicted by what one might call the 'Socrates complex'. The symptoms are various: a lack of historical awareness, a disparagement of the senses and the body, a concomitant

---

[26] Cf. Daniel W. Conway, 'Nietzsche's *Doppelgänger*: Affirmation and Resentment in *Ecce Homo*', in *The Fate of the New Nietzsche*, ed. Keith Ansell-Pearson and Howard Caygill (Aldershot and Brookfield, Vt.: Avebury, 1993), 55–78.

privileging of abstractions such as 'being' and 'God' (reinforced by the metaphysics inherent in language itself), and an erroneous conception of causality underpinned by an inverted temporality (this last a major theme which is introduced here and will be developed throughout section VI). In 'Maxims and Barbs' Nietzsche was keen to counterbalance his negative psychological observations by interspersing them with a number of passages promoting qualities he would count as virtues, such as strength in adversity (I 8), heroic isolation (I 14), or immoralism (I 36), and then ending the section on a decidedly upbeat note (I 42–4); here again we find a specific moment of perspectival inversion (III 5) when he deliberately switches over from the description and denunciation of errors to a 'superior' perspective which is advocated in their place. This rapid reversal of polarity from negative to positive towards the end of a section is a typical move, since for Nietzsche destruction is but the prelude to creation.[27] As he will put it later on: 'We do not readily deny; we seek our honour in being *affirmative*' (V 6; cf. VIII 6), and by means of such peripeteias he carefully organizes the rhythmic structure of his text to bear this aspiration out.

' "Reason" in Philosophy' shows as great an awareness of the reader as ever: it begins as a response to an imagined question and concludes schematically with its main points reduced to four short summarizing propositions. The compression of this last paragraph is maintained and indeed surpassed in the next section, 'How the "Real World" Finally Became a Fable', a (minimally) extended gloss on it. The 'error' whose vicissitudes Nietzsche tracks over the brief span of this page-long 'history' (or 'story': 'Geschichte') is that of conceiving the 'real world' as divorced from and opposed to the empirical world of sense-perception, and in turn downgrading the latter to the status of mere 'appearance'. Nietzsche here encapsulates his critique of metaphysics with breathtaking succinctness: short sections of statement alternate with parenthetic commentary couched in mischievously parabolic terms as he passes in quick succession from Plato through Christianity, Kant, and nineteenth-century positivism to his own creations, the 'free spirits' (the 'self-legislators' who have liberated themselves from previous moral prejudices—cf. HA I, 'Preface')

[27] In addition to I 42–4 and III 5, cf. IV 6; V 6; VI 8; IX 48–51. Sections VIII and X differ from this pattern only in the sense that they begin and end on a positive note (cf. VIII 1, 6–7; X 1, 4–5).

and Zarathustra (founder of the dualistic religion of Zoroastrianism whom Nietzsche, from *Thus Spake Zarathustra* onwards, takes 'beyond good and evil' as a fictional symbol of the 'self-overcoming of morality'). This section has rightly become one of the most famous passages in Nietzsche's whole *œuvre*: he himself (never one to underestimate his own achievements) certainly appreciated its cogency, for it had been destined to open the first book of *The Will to Power* (KSA 14, 415), and Martin Heidegger was to write of it: 'here, in a magnificent moment of vision, the entire realm of Nietzsche's thought is permeated by a new and singular brilliance.'[28] It is not surprising that Nietzsche should have been adopted as a crucial precursor by post-structuralist philosophers, for this short section provides an object lesson in the deconstruction of a binary opposition—in Nietzsche's eyes the most ingrained and mystificatory of all.

After this inspired interlude, Nietzsche returns to the more moderate pace of the previous two sections, and to a more sustained unmasking of philosophical error from a predominantly psychological standpoint: the stylistic caesura is bridged by the continuity of thematic concerns. Because of his decision to develop his material on Christianity into a separate book, *The Antichrist*, relatively little on this topic remains in *Twilight*, and it is concentrated in sections V–VII. In 'Morality as Anti-Nature', Nietzsche focuses for the first time in this text on Christian morality (as '*inimical to life*'—V 1), developing arguments from *On the Genealogy of Morals*, and especially its Third Essay, 'What is the Meaning of Ascetic Ideals?', in which he had highlighted the polymorphous perversity of the human will which 'would even will *nothingness* rather than *not* will at all' (GM III 1). Christian morality is criticized here in familiar terms, as a symptom of decadence (V 5), a 'degenerates' idiosyncrasy' (V 6); specifically it is dismissed on the same grounds as Socratic dialectics previously (II 11)—for being anti-instinctual, in Freudian terms the product of a repression—and its apologists are unmasked as the enemies of sensuality (cf. III 1), what Zarathustra had called 'Des-

---

[28] Heidegger, 'Nietzsche's Overturning of Platonism', in *Nietzsche, Volume I: The Will to Power as Art*, trans. David Farrell Krell (London and Henley: Routledge & Kegan Paul, 1981), 202. For responses to Heidegger's reading of this passage, cf. Jacques Derrida, 'Histoire d'une erreur'/'History of an Error' and 'Femina Vita', in *Spurs*, 70-95, and Alan D. Schrift, *Nietzsche and the Question of Interpretation: Between Hermeneutics and Deconstruction* (New York and London: Routledge, 1990), 46-9.

pisers of the Body' (Z I; cf. IX 47). Nietzsche here outlines two
contrasting ways of dealing with the passions: the Christian way
(abnegation, asceticism, excision) and 'our' way (V 3)—'spiritualization' (Freud will pick up on another of Nietzsche's formulations
(HA I 1) and say 'sublimation'). But Nietzsche is careful to point out
that the answer to the Christian perversion is not to excise it in turn,
for it provides a necessary counterpole to his own prescriptions: even
immoralists need a morality in place (cf. I 36). Whereas Christianity
craves the dissolution of oppositional forces in 'perpetual peace' (and
Kant, author of a treatise with that title, has already been dismissed
as 'a *crafty* Christian, when all's said and done'—III 6), Nietzsche
argues here for 'the value of having enemies' (V 3), the necessity of
opposition and war.

Although the title of the next section, 'The Four Great Errors',
might lead one to expect a relatively diverse discussion, it is in fact a
sustained critique of the common conception of causality as the basis
of all previous moralities and metaphysics: the last three 'errors'—
'false causality', 'imaginary causes', 'free will'—are but subspecies of
the first, the 'confusion of cause and consequence'.[29] Man's falsifying
'causal drive', Nietzsche argues here (VI 4), has vitiated our understanding of the world thus far by opening up an erroneous 'inner
world' of volition, consciousness, and subjectivity (VI 3; cf. GM
II 16), which he dispatches with as much relish as he had earlier
shown in disposing of its analogue, the will-o'-the-wisp 'real world'.
His arguments for the necessity of a correct historical awareness
become more narrowly focused here on a fundamental error at the
microlevel of psychological temporality: 'causes' are in reality only
after-effects 'foisted on' to events, after the event, in a 'chronological
reversal' (VI 4) prompted by the desperate human need for explanation at any price. So although Nietzsche develops the trope of
'inversion' throughout *Twilight* in predominantly topological
terms—'overturning' that which was hitherto 'topsy-turvy', restoring things to their rightful place—'The Four Great Errors', at the
heart of the text, reminds us that the most chronic of philosophy's
illnesses is *chronological* in nature.

[29] The plural title may well have been intended as a tribute to the four 'Idols of
the Mind' proposed by Nietzsche's Elizabethan forebear Francis Bacon (whom he
honoured as the 'real' author of Shakespeare's plays—EH II 4) in his *Novum Organum*
(1620), i. 39–44.

Towards the end of this section (VI 7) Nietzsche rehearses the conspiracy theory he had presented in *On the Genealogy of Morals*—that the myth of human 'free will' was originally fabricated by resentful priests seeking to take revenge on their flock by making them succumb to 'guilt' and 'bad conscience' (GM II). As he warms to his theme, the stridency of his invective increases: the section climaxes in the starkest possible condemnation of Christianity, as a 'metaphysics of the hangman' (VI 7), before concluding with an outright denial of God which confirms the madman's proclamation of 'the death of God' in *The Gay Science* (GS 125). But an Antichrist's work is never done, and just as the madman is forced to acknowledge that there are all too many still willing to treat the report of God's death as an exaggeration, so Nietzsche presses on, for there are always more egregious Christian errors to correct.

Appropriately enough, he turns next to those who would themselves 'correct' humanity (or 'improve' it—the German 'Verbesserer' means both). At two previous points Nietzsche had rounded on moral prescriptivists, first arguing that '*the entire morality of improvement, Christianity's included, was a misunderstanding*' (II 11) and then exasperatedly explaining 'what naïvety it is in general to say "man *should* be such and such!"' (V 6), for an individual's character is the necessary consequence of an irreversible series of past events, so that to attempt to change that 'piece of fate' is in effect to demand another impossible chronological reversal: 'Telling him to change means demanding that everything should change, even backwards...' (V 6). In 'The "Improvers" of Humanity' Nietzsche goes in pursuit of these counterfactual counterfeiters, distinguishing between two kinds: those who have sought to 'tame' man, such as the Christian priests, and those whose aim has been rather to 'breed' a specific 'race' of men, such as the author of the *Law of Manu*, the foremost moral code of the Hindus. Nietzsche's preference for the 'healthier, higher, *wider* world' of the latter is evident—'How miserable the "New Testament" is compared to Manu, how badly it smells!' (VII 3)—but it is crucial to note that for Nietzsche Manu is still a charlatan, a 'pious fraud' (VII 5), even if a nobler, more distinguished one. This exercise in comparative religion may serve to focus Nietzsche's disgust at the perversity of Christianity, which, echoing his analysis of 'the slave revolt in morals' in the *Genealogy* (GM I 10), he brands 'the *counter-movement* to any morality of breeding, of

pedigree, of privilege' (VII 4), but it is also very far from an endorse-
ment of 'Aryan humaneness' (VII 4), and the irony behind his use of
this latter term to describe the gruesome prohibitions inflicted on the
lowest order of Hindu society is made perfectly apparent in the
following sentence when he encloses it in inverted commas.
Nietzsche is sailing quite close to the wind here, but it would be a
gross misreading to see this section as lending support, for example,
to the programme of eugenics put into practice by the National
Socialists—who were so keen to appropriate Nietzsche as their
philosophical forerunner—when it argues exactly the opposite.
'The last thing *I* should promise would be to improve humanity',
Nietzsche states categorically in *Ecce Homo* (EH, 'Preface' 2), and on
the evidence of this section we should believe him.

Having analysed successively the decadence of the ancient Greeks,
of Western post-Socratic philosophy, and of Christianity, in section
VIII, 'What the Germans Lack', Nietzsche turns his attention to the
decadence of his fellow-countrymen (although he had actually
renounced his Prussian citizenship on moving to Basle in 1869, two
years before Germany's unification, so he never had 'German nation-
ality' as such). This section began life after the rest of the first draft as
a Foreword—confirming the fact that, for all Nietzsche's efforts to
find translators for the work, its principal addressees are the Germans
themselves—but it soon outgrew its initially modest dimensions and
was granted a place in the main text. The answer to the implicit
question posed by the section title can be summed up very succinctly
in German with the single word 'Geist' (mind, intellect, spirit), on
which the section as a whole is a set of bravura variations: the word
itself, together with the six derivatives Nietzsche uses, occurs no
fewer than twenty-four times. Although at first sight this section
might seem quite a departure from the book's earlier concerns, as
though Nietzsche could not resist taking one last swipe at his
unfortunate compatriots, it takes its cue from his critique of the
anti-intellectualism of the early Christian church (V 1), and the
priests' domestication of 'the noble Teutons' in particular (VII 2).
Nietzsche returns here to the themes of his early phase of cultural
criticism in the first half of the 1870s: as in his first *Untimely Meditation*, he lambastes Germany's preoccupation with *realpolitik* at the
expense of its intellectual, philosophical, and cultural pre-eminence;
as in his early lecture series 'On the Future of our Educational

Institutions' (1872), he adopts an unashamedly élitist position, targeting in particular the massification of the German education system and the debasement of its humanistic ideal of all-round education ('Bildung').

Nietzsche's alarm at the 'dumbing down' of a national culture will strike many today as familiar, although his diagnosis of the factors jointly responsible for this decline is inimitable: 'the two great European narcotics, alcohol and Christianity' (VIII 2), together with 'our constipated, constipating German music' (for which read 'Wagner'). The diatribe against beer-drinking which Nietzsche gives us here might seem plain cranky, but it is more than just a provocation, for it is perfectly in accord with what one might call his 'somatopsychic' principle, that mental debilitation derives directly from physiological affliction (cf. IX 31). In *Ecce Homo* he will have more to say on 'the origin of the *German spirit*—from distressed intestines' (EH II 1); here, typically, he turns at the end of the section to his patent remedy: the philosophy teacher must emulate the dancing master and seek to promote '*light feet* in intellectual matters' (VIII 7; cf. VI 2). Then, as if immediately to demonstrate that he can more than hold his own on the philosophical dance-floor, he opens the next section with a series of dazzling stylistic pirouettes, a catalogue of 'My Impossibles' (IX 1) which outstrips even sections I and IV in its epigrammatic allusiveness.

'Reconnaissance Raids of an Untimely Man' was originally planned as two sections, entitled 'Among Artists and Writers' (1–18) and 'From My Aesthetics' (19–31, 45–51), but in October 1888, while correcting the proofs, Nietzsche inserted the material for paragraphs 32–44 (once more from material originally intended for *The Will to Power*) and combined all three sections into one. As a result it is by far the longest section in *Twilight*—taking up almost half the book—and it is correspondingly the most diverse, mixing stylistic and thematic elements from all the previous sections. As in 'Maxims and Barbs', here there are further psychological observations of a general kind—on 'impersonality' (IX 15, 28), hypocrisy (IX 18, 42), egoism (IX 33), altruism (IX 35)—although they are worked through at greater length than their earlier counterparts. As in 'The Problem of Socrates', we find critical character portraits, now generally confined to single paragraphs (IX 2, 3, 5, 6, 12), interspersed with occasional gibes at the expense of philosophical opponents such as Rousseau (IX 1, 3, 6, 48) and Kant (IX 1, 16, 29, 42, 49); moreover, Nietzsche periodically returns to his battle with Christianity (IX 2, 4, 5, 34), and with Christian morality in particular (IX 5, 24, 37).

After concentrating on 'eternal idols' so far, though, here Nietzsche goes roaming in the gloaming of predominantly 'contemporary idols', darting into their lugubrious expanse from the margins of contemporaneity where 'the view is clear' (IX 46). And he turns for the first time in this text to two subjects about which he has so far said relatively little: aesthetics and politics. ' "Reason" in Philosophy' had ended with a thumbnail sketch of the tragic, Dionysian artist affirming life in the raw, as a counter-example to the anaemic anti-vitalism of the metaphysical dualists (III 6). Here Nietzsche explains in more detail what he means by the Dionysian state—a feeling of intoxication, of plenitude and power (IX 8–9)—and he surveys the individual forms of artistic expression, from the contemplative and hence 'Apollonian' visual arts through the more physically involving 'Dionysian' arts of music and dance (IX 10), to architecture, which he now considers the best realization of 'great style' in art: 'a kind of power-eloquence in forms' (IX 11). By granting architecture such a privileged role, Nietzsche shows how far away he has moved from the aesthetic hierarchy of his early mentor Schopenhauer— who placed architecture on the lowest rung of the ladder[30]—and from his own Schopenhauer-inspired first book, *The Birth of Tragedy*. Indeed he explicitly criticizes Schopenhauer for perpetrating 'the greatest piece of psychological counterfeiting in history, Christianity excepted' (IX 21), by interpreting art in general as a denial of the will, and of the procreative urge above all (IX 22), when for him art is the exact opposite, 'the great stimulant to life' (IX 24).

On the political front, Nietzsche in this section gives a conspectus of practically all the salient theories and movements of his day— social Darwinism (IX 14), anarchism, egalitarianism, socialism, and the labour movement (IX 30, 34, 37, 40, 48), liberalism, nationalism, and parliamentary democracy (IX 37–9)—spelling out his resistance to each in turn. The advocates of these doctrines are revealed to be

---

[30] Cf. Arthur Schopenhauer, *The World as Will and Representation*, 2 vols., trans. E. F. J. Payne (New York: Dover, 1966), i. 43–52.

simply those old foes the ' "improvers" of humanity' in secularized garb; their 'modern ideas' encapsulate the shallow meliorism of a decadent age which has failed to grasp that the only way to 'progress' is to go 'step by step further in décadence' (IX 43). Nietzsche's own idea of progress is a very different one: he envisages history not as the ascent of man toward the glittering heights of some gimcrack new Jerusalem, but rather as a succession of long periods of mediocrity punctuated by forceful explosions which give birth to such exemplary individuals as Caesar and Napoleon (IX 38, 44–5, 48). This profoundly anti-Hegelian view of history can be traced right back to the earliest phase of Nietzsche's career, when he had argued in the second *Untimely Meditation* (1874) that 'the *goal of humanity* cannot lie in its end but only *in its highest exemplars*' (UM II 9). In the meantime, as we have seen, he may have moved away in many respects from the philosophy of his 'educator' Schopenhauer (UM III), including Schopenhauer's conception of the cultural role of the genius (IX 21), but in thematizing and valorizing the genius *per se* he remains a Romantic Schopenhauerian to the last.

A notable absentee from Nietzsche's roll-call of decadent 'modern ideas' in this section is the contemporary women's movement in Germany, his abhorrence for which he had already made abundantly clear elsewhere (BGE 239), although his silence on this topic is more than compensated for by the persistence of a casual and at times deliberately outrageous misogyny (another inheritance from Schopenhauer), as in the collocation: 'shopkeepers, Christians, cows, women, Englishmen, and other democrats' (IX 38). Women writers such as George Sand (IX 1, 6) and George Eliot (IX 5) are inevitably abused as women, as examples of that comical *curiosum* 'the literary woman' (IX 27; cf. I 20), whose practice Nietzsche might well have likened to a dog's walking on his hinder legs had not Samuel Johnson got there before him. Among the writers and thinkers (of either sex) whom Nietzsche discusses over the course of this voluminous section, very few emerge with honour: Emerson (IX 13), Dostoevsky (IX 45), the handful of dead Germans whom Nietzsche permits to be counted as 'European events' (IX 21). But pre-eminent among all these is the titanic figure of Goethe, for whom Nietzsche is unashamed to declare his outright 'reverence' (IX 51) in the last four paragraphs of the section, where he sings a last great hymn of praise to this Dionysian artist incarnate (IX 49), the proto-'overman' against whom he had always implicitly measured himself.

Nietzsche had initially intended to close the book with these 'Raids', which is why the last of them (IX 51) seems such an appropriate place to end—even if, like the Foreword, its final words act as a cliff-hanging trailer for the 'Revaluation', teasing the reader by announcing: 'There cometh one mightier than I after me.' But in October 1888 he inserted an extra section from the material he was by this stage already composing for *Ecce Homo*—hence the first-person reference in the title, 'What I Owe the Ancients', which prefigures the 'Why I Am So Wise', 'Why I Am So Clever', 'Why I Write Such Good Books', and 'Why I Am a Destiny' of the later text. His reason for making this addition would seem to be primarily structural, since by devoting the last main section in the book to his own philosophical and stylistic inheritances from classical writers, Nietzsche returns us to 'the problem of Socrates' (this time considered from the perspective of Plato's deficiencies as a stylist), and by closing with references to his first book, *The Birth of Tragedy*, he closes the circle on his whole philosophical career thus far, confirming the recapitulative nature of *Twilight* as a whole. These recursive structures neatly illustrate the philosophical principle whose first announcement in this text Nietzsche delays till as late as the last two paragraphs of this section: 'the eternal return', Zarathustra's 'most abyssal thought' that all things recur endlessly (VIII 4–5; cf. Z III, 'Of the Vision and the Riddle'). The text was still not complete, though, for at the last minute Nietzsche grafted on a coda, 'The Hammer Speaks', a slightly modified excerpt from *Thus Spake Zarathustra* itself which he had been intending to use as a conclusion to *The Antichrist* (cf. KSA 14, 454). He thus rounds off the book with yet another element of stylistic variety, the mock-biblical poetry of his 'favourite son', which returns us to the hammer imagery of the text's subtitle and Foreword and at the same time stresses one final time the continuity of his work as a whole, Goethe's 'permanence in change'.

Conclusion

In a letter to his Leipzig publisher Naumann on 7 September 1888, Nietzsche expressed the hope that *Twilight* might perhaps 'open people's ears to me a little' (KGB III/5, 412), and if one considers the book in the musical terms which he favoured, then with its 'horrible detonations'[31] it does indeed resemble that most celebrated of all orchestral ear-openers, Tchaikovsky's *1812* Overture. Yet at the same time it has the character of something altogether more intimate—a chamber piece, or perhaps a nocturne by Nietzsche's namesake and would-be fellow-countryman Fryderyk Chopin.[32] If these two qualities are combined, the picture which emerges is of a Nietzsche seeking to emulate another namesake, Frederick the Great—not whiling away his time between wars on the flute at Sans-Souci, but spending his 'psychologist's idleness' hammering out a medley of his best tunes on his own preferred instrument, the piano. In the finale of his Sixth ('Tragic') Symphony Gustav Mahler, one of the most Nietzschean of composers, introduces an actual hammer into his orchestration, to depict 'the hero on whom three blows of fate descend, the last of which fells him like a tree'. But just as Mahler was diagnosed with a fatal heart condition only a year after the symphony's first performance, so Nietzsche was felled by his own hammer-blow of fate barely six weeks after receiving the first pre-publication copies of *Twilight*. The book was eventually published on 24 January 1889, but on 3 January its author had collapsed into the perpetual twilight of insanity.

[31] Letter to Heinrich Köselitz, 27 Sept. 1888 (KGB III/5, 443).
[32] For an ingenious analysis of the work in musical terms, cf. Michael Allen Gillespie, 'Nietzsche's Musical Politics', in *Nietzsche's New Seas: Explorations in Philosophy, Aesthetics, and Politics*, ed. Michael Allen Gillespie and Tracy B. Strong (Chicago and London: University of Chicago Press, 1988), 117–49.

NOTE ON THE TRANSLATION

The text on which this translation is based is the standard German edition, *Götzen-Dämmerung oder Wie man mit dem Hammer philoso-phirt*, prepared by Giorgio Colli and Mazzino Montinari (KGW VI/3, 49–157). In writing the notes I have benefited from consulting the notes to the Colli–Montinari *Kritische Studienausgabe* and to Peter Pütz's 'Goldmann Klassiker' edition (Munich, 1988). In addition to glossing Nietzsche's references and allusions I have tried to alert the reader to any linguistic play which could not be adequately conveyed by the translation itself, to provide as many cross-references within the text as might be useful, and to relate its arguments and stylistic features to those of Nietzsche's other works.

I should like to thank Jim Reed for his helpful suggestions at an early stage in the translation; my colleagues Tom Cheesman and Rolf Jucker, with whom I discussed parts of the final draft; my copy-editor, Jeff New, for his meticulous attentiveness; and above all my editors Catherine Clarke, Susie Casement, Judith Luna, and Joanna Rabiger for their unfailingly patient support.

SELECT BIBLIOGRAPHY

On *Twilight of the Idols*

Gillespie, Michael Allen, 'Nietzsche's Musical Politics', in Michael Allen Gillespie and Tracy B. Strong (eds.), *Nietzsche's New Seas: Explorations in Philosophy, Aesthetics, and Politics* (Chicago and London: University of Chicago Press, 1988), 117–49.

Magnus, Bernd, 'The Deification of the Commonplace: *Twilight of the Idols*', in Robert C. Solomon and Kathleen M. Higgins (eds.), *Reading Nietzsche* (New York and Oxford: Oxford University Press, 1988), 152–81.

——— Stewart, Stanley, and Mileur, Jean-Pierre, 'Post(pre)face: The Body of Thought Redux', in *Nietzsche's Case: Philosophy as/and Literature* (New York and London: Routledge, 1993), 234–55.

Young, Julian, '*Twilight of the Idols*', in *Nietzsche's Philosophy of Art* (Cambridge: Cambridge University Press, 1992), 117–47.

Twilight in Context

Allison, David B. (ed.), *The New Nietzsche: Contemporary Styles of Interpretation*, 2nd edn. (Cambridge, Mass., and London: MIT Press, 1985).

Burgard, Peter J. (ed.), *Nietzsche and the Feminine* (Charlottesville: University Press of Virginia, 1994).

Conway, Daniel W., *Nietzsche and the Political* (London and New York: Routledge, 1997).

Deleuze, Gilles, *Nietzsche and Philosophy*, trans. Hugh Tomlinson (London: Athlone Press; New York: Columbia University Press, 1983).

Hayman, Ronald, *Nietzsche: A Critical Life* (London: Weidenfeld and Nicolson, 1980).

Hollingdale, R. J., *Nietzsche: The Man and His Philosophy* (London: Routledge & Kegan Paul, 1965).

Kaufmann, Walter, *Nietzsche: Philosopher, Psychologist, Antichrist*, 4th edn. (Princeton: Princeton University Press, 1974).

Kofman, Sarah, *Nietzsche and Metaphor*, trans. Duncan Large (London: Athlone Press; Stanford: Stanford University Press, 1993).

Magnus, Bernd, and Higgins, Kathleen M. (eds.), *The Cambridge Companion to Nietzsche* (Cambridge: Cambridge University Press, 1996).

Nehamas, Alexander, *Nietzsche: Life as Literature* (Cambridge, Mass., and London: Harvard University Press, 1985).

Parkes, Graham, *Composing the Soul: Reaches of Nietzsche's Psychology* (Chicago and London: University of Chicago Press, 1994).

Pasley, Malcolm (ed.), *Nietzsche: Imagery and Thought* (London: Methuen, 1978).

Schacht, Richard, *Nietzsche* (London: Routledge & Kegan Paul, 1983).

Stern, J. P., *Nietzsche* (London: Fontana, 1978).

A CHRONOLOGY OF FRIEDRICH NIETZSCHE

1844   Friedrich Wilhelm Nietzsche born in Röcken (Saxony) on 15 October, son of Karl Ludwig and Franziska Nietzsche. His father and both grandfathers are Protestant clergymen.

1846   Birth of sister Elisabeth.

1849   Birth of brother Joseph; death of father.

1850   Death of brother; family moves to Naumburg.

1858–64 Attends renowned boys' boarding-school Pforta, where he excels in classics. Begins to suffer from migraine attacks which will plague him for the rest of his career.

1864   Enters Bonn University to study theology and classical philology.

1865   Follows classics professor Ritschl to Leipzig University, where he drops theology and continues with studies in classical philology. Discovers Schopenhauer's philosophy and becomes a passionate admirer.

1867   Begins publishing career with essay on Theognis; continues publishing philological articles and book reviews till 1873.

1867–8 Military service in Naumburg, until invalided out after a riding accident.

1868   Back in Leipzig, meets Richard Wagner for the first time and quickly becomes a devotee. Increasing disaffection with philology: plans to escape to Paris to study chemistry.

1869   On Ritschl's recommendation, appointed Extraordinary Professor of Classical Philology at Basle University. Awarded doctorate without examination; renounces Prussian citizenship. Begins a series of idyllic visits to the Wagners at Tribschen, on Lake Lucerne. Develops admiration for Jacob Burckhardt, his new colleague in Basle.

1870   Promoted to full professor. Participates in Franco–Prussian War as volunteer medical orderly, but contracts dysentery and diphtheria at the front within a fortnight.

1871   Granted semester's sick leave from Basle and works intensively on *The Birth of Tragedy*. Germany unified; founding of the Reich.

1872   Publishes *The Birth of Tragedy out of the Spirit of Music*, which earns him the condemnation of professional colleagues. Lectures 'On the Future of our Educational Institutions'; attends laying of foundation stone for Bayreuth Festival Theatre.

1873   Publishes first *Untimely Meditation: David Strauss the Confessor and the Writer*.

1874   Publishes second and third *Untimely Meditations: On the Use and Disadvantage of History for Life* and *Schopenhauer as Educator*. Relationship with Wagner begins to sour.

1875   Meets musician Heinrich Köselitz (Peter Gast), who idolizes him.

1876   Publishes fourth and last *Untimely Meditation: Richard Wagner in Bayreuth*. Attends first Bayreuth Festival but leaves early and subsequently breaks with Wagner. Further illness; granted full year's sick leave from the university.

1877   French translation of *Richard Wagner in Bayreuth* published, the only translation to appear during his mentally active lifetime.

1878   Publishes *Human, All Too Human: A Book for Free Spirits*, which confirms the break with Wagner.

1879   Publishes supplement to *Human, All Too Human, Assorted Opinions and Maxims*. Finally retires from teaching on a pension; first visits the Engadine, summering in St Moritz.

1880   Publishes *The Wanderer and His Shadow*. First stays in Venice and Genoa.

1881   Publishes *Daybreak: Thoughts on the Prejudices of Morality*. First stay in Sils-Maria.

1882   Publishes *The Gay Science*. Infatuation with Lou Andreas-Salomé, who spurns his marriage proposals.

1883   Publishes *Thus Spake Zarathustra: A Book for Everyone and No One*, Parts I and II (separately). Death of Wagner. Spends the summer in Sils and the winter in Nice, his pattern for the next five years. Increasingly consumed by writing.

1884   Publishes *Thus Spake Zarathustra*, Part III.

1885   *Thus Spake Zarathustra*, Part IV printed but circulated to only a handful of friends. Begins in earnest to amass notes for *The Will to Power*.

1886   Publishes *Beyond Good and Evil: Prelude to a Philosophy of the Future*. Change of publisher results in new expanded editions of

The Birth of Tragedy and *Human, All Too Human* (now with a second volume comprising the *Assorted Opinions and Maxims* and *The Wanderer and His Shadow*).

1887   Publishes *On the Genealogy of Morals: A Polemic*. New expanded editions of *Daybreak* and *The Gay Science*.

1888   Begins to receive public recognition: Georg Brandes lectures on his work in Copenhagen. Discovers Turin, where he writes *The Wagner Case: A Musician's Problem*. Abandons *The Will to Power*, then completes in quick succession: *Twilight of the Idols, or How to Philosophize with a Hammer* (first published 1889), *The Antichrist: Curse on Christianity* (f.p. 1895), *Ecce Homo, or How One Becomes What One Is* (f.p. 1908), *Nietzsche contra Wagner: Documents of a Psychologist* (f.p. 1895), and *Dionysus Dithyrambs* (f.p. 1892).

1889   Suffers mental breakdown in Turin (3 January) and is eventually committed to asylum in Jena. *Twilight of the Idols* published 24 January, the first of his new books to appear after his collapse.

1890   Discharged into the care of his mother in Naumburg.

1894   Elisabeth founds Nietzsche Archive in Naumburg (moving it to Weimar two years later).

1897   Mother dies; Elisabeth moves her brother to Weimar.

1900   Friedrich Nietzsche dies in Weimar on 25 August.

TWILIGHT OF THE IDOLS*

or

How to Philosophize
with a Hammer*

FOREWORD

In the midst of a gloomy and exceedingly responsible business it is quite some trick to keep cheerful: and yet, what could be more necessary than cheerfulness?* Nothing succeeds without high spirits playing their part. Excess of strength is the sole proof of strength.—A *revaluation of all values*,* this question mark so black, so immense, that it casts a shadow over the one who sets it down—such a destiny of a task forces you to run out into the sunshine every instant and shake off a heavy, all-too-heavy seriousness.* Any means will do, every 'case' is a stroke of luck.* Above all *war*. War has always been the great ruse of all spirits grown too inward, too profound; even a wound has healing power. A maxim whose provenance I withhold from scholarly curiosity has long been my motto:

*increscunt animi, virescit volnere virtus.**

A different convalescence, possibly even more desirable to me, is *to sound out idols* . . . There are more idols than realities in the world: that is *my* 'evil eye' for this world; it is also my 'evil *ear*' . . . Here for once to ask questions with a *hammer* and, perhaps, to hear in response that famous hollow sound which speaks of swollen innards—what a delight for one who has ears even behind his ears, for the old psychologist and Pied Piper that I am, who makes the very things that would rather keep quiet *pipe up** . . .

This work, too*—the title betrays it*—is above all a recuperation, a sunspot, a sideways leap into the idleness of a psychologist. Perhaps also a new war? And are new idols being sounded out? . . . This little work is a *great declaration of war*;* and as far as sounding out idols is concerned, this time it is not contemporary idols but *eternal* idols that are being touched here with a hammer as if with a tuning fork—there simply are no more ancient, more convinced, more puffed-up idols . . . Nor any hollower ones . . . That does not prevent them being the *most believed in*; and by no means, especially in the most distinguished case, do people say 'idol' . . .

Turin, 30 September 1888, the day the first book of the *Revaluation of All Values** came to an end.

Friedrich Nietzsche

MAXIMS AND BARBS*

1

Psychology finds work for idle hands to do.* What? does that make psychology a—devil?

2

Even the bravest of us only rarely has the courage for what he actually *knows* . . .

3

To live alone you must be an animal or a god—says Aristotle.* He left out the third case: you must be both—*a philosopher* . . .

4

'All truth is simple.'—Is that not a compound lie?*—

5

I want, once and for all, *not* to know many things.—Wisdom sets limits even to knowledge.

6

You recover best in your wild nature from your unnaturalness, your intellectuality . . .

7

What? is man just one of God's mistakes? Or is God just one of man's?—

8

From the Military School of Life.—Whatever does not kill me makes me stronger.*

9

Everyone else helps those who help themselves. Principle of brotherly love.

10

Do not be cowardly towards your actions! Do not abandon them after the event!—Remorse is indecent.*

11

Can an *ass** be tragic?—Perishing under a load you can neither bear nor shed? . . . The case of the philosopher.

12

If you have your *why?* for life, then you can get along with almost any *how?*—Man does *not* strive for happiness; only the English do that.*

13

Man created woman—but from what? From a rib of his God*—of his 'ideal' . . .

14

What? you are searching? you would like to multiply yourself by ten, by a hundred? you are looking for followers?—Look for *zeros*!*—

15

Posthumous people—like me, for example—are less well understood than timely ones,* but better *heard*. More strictly: we are never understood—and *hence* our authority . . .

16

Among Women.—'Truth? Oh you don't know truth! Isn't it an attempt on all our *pudeurs*?'*—

17

That is the kind of artist I like, modest in his needs; he actually wants only two things: his bread and his art—*panem et* Circen*...

18

Anyone who cannot manage to invest his will in things at least invests them with a *meaning*: i.e. he believes there is already a will in them (principle of 'belief').

19

What? you chose virtue and puffed-out chests, and at the same time are looking enviously at the advantages of the inconsiderate?—But with virtue one *dispenses* with 'advantages'...(for an anti-Semite's front door).

20

The complete woman commits literature as she commits a little sin:* to try it out, in passing, looking round to see if anyone has noticed and *so that* someone will notice...

21

Put yourself only in situations where you are not allowed any false virtues and where instead, like the tightrope walker* on his rope, you either fall or stand—or get away...

22

'Wicked people have no songs.'*—How come the Russians* have songs?

23

'German spirit':* for the last eighteen years* a contradiction in terms.

24

To search for beginnings you turn into a crab. The historian looks backwards; in the end he even *believes* backwards.

25

Contentment protects you even from catching cold. Did any woman who knew she was well-dressed ever catch cold?—I am assuming she was scantily clad.

26

I mistrust all systematists and avoid them. The will to system is a lack of integrity.

27

People think woman is profound—why? because you can never get to the bottom of her. Woman is not even shallow.

28

If a woman has manly virtues you should run away from her; and if she has no manly virtues she runs away herself.

29

'How many remorsels did the conscience have to bite on in former times? what good teeth did it have?—And today? what's missing?'—a dentist's question.*

30

Rash actions are rarely one-offs. With the first rash action people always do too much. Which is precisely why they usually commit a second—when they do too little . . .

31

A worm squirms when it is trodden on.* Clever move. By doing so it reduces the probability of being trodden on again. In the language of morality: *humility*.—

32

There is a hatred of lying and pretence which comes from a sensitive notion of honour; there is exactly the same sort of hatred which comes from cowardice, in so far as lying is *forbidden* by a divine command. Too cowardly to lie . . .

33

How little it takes to be happy! The sound of bagpipes.—Without music life would be a mistake. The Germans even think of God as singing songs.*

34

On ne peut penser et écrire qu'assis* (G. Flaubert).*—Now I've got you, you nihilist!* Sitting still is precisely the *sin* against the holy ghost. Only thoughts which come from *walking* have any value.

35

There are times when we are like horses, we psychologists, and get restive: we see our own shadows in front of us fluctuating up and down. The psychologist has to look away from *himself* to see anything at all.

36

Do we immoralists* do virtue any *harm*?—Just as little as anarchists* do to princes. Only since these latter have been shot at have they been sitting tight on their thrones again. Moral: *we must shoot at morality*.

37

You are running on *ahead*?—Are you doing it as a shepherd? or as an exception? A third case would be the runaway . . . *First* question for the conscience.

38

Are you genuine? or just a play-actor? A representative? or the actual thing represented?—Ultimately you are even just an imitation play-actor . . . *Second* question for the conscience.

39

The *disillusioned man speaks.*—I was looking for great human beings;
I only ever found the *apes* of their ideal.*

40

Are you one who looks on? or who lends a hand?—or who looks away,
sidles off? ... *Third* question for the conscience.

41

Do you want to go along with others? or go on ahead? or go off on
your own? ... You must know *what* you want and *that* you want.
Fourth question for the conscience.

42

Those were steps for me; I climbed up by way of them—and so had to
pass beyond them. But they thought I wanted to sit down and rest on
them ...

43

What does it matter that *I* turn out to be right! I *am* too often right.—
And he who laughs longest today also laughs last.

44

Formula for my happiness: a yes, a no, a straight line, a *goal** ...

THE PROBLEM OF SOCRATES*

I

Throughout the ages the wisest of men have passed the same judgement on life: *it is no good*... Always and everywhere their mouths have been heard to produce the same sound—a sound full of doubt, full of melancholy, full of weariness of life, full of resistance to life. Even Socrates said as he was dying: 'Life is one long illness: I owe the saviour Asclepius a cock.'* Even Socrates had had enough of it.— What does this *prove*? What does this *point to*?—In former times people would have said (—oh they did say it, and loudly enough, with our pessimists* in the vanguard!): 'There must be at least something true here! The *consensus sapientium** proves the truth.'—Shall we still speak in such terms today? *can* we do so? 'There must be at least something *sick* here' is the answer *we* give: these wisest of every age,* we should look at them from close to! Were they all perhaps no longer steady on their feet? belated? doddery? *décadents*?* Would wisdom perhaps appear on earth as a raven excited by a faint whiff of carrion?...

2

I myself was first struck by this impertinent thought, that the great wise men are *declining types*, in the very case where it meets with its strongest opposition from scholarly and unscholarly prejudice: I recognized Socrates and Plato as symptoms of decay, as tools of the Greek dissolution, as pseudo-Greek, as anti-Greek (*Birth of Tragedy*, 1872).* That *consensus sapientium*—I have realized it more and more—proves least of all that they were right in what they agreed on: it proves rather that they themselves, these wisest of men, were somehow in *physiological* agreement in order to have—to *have* to have—the same negative attitude towards life. Judgements, value judgements on life, whether for or against, can ultimately never be true: they have value only as symptoms, they can be considered only as symptoms—in themselves such judgements are foolish. We must really stretch out our fingers and make the effort to grasp this astonishing *finesse*, *that the value of life cannot be assessed.** Not by a living person because he is an interested party, indeed even the object of dispute, and not the judge; nor by a dead person, for a different reason. For a philosopher to see a problem in the *value* of life is thus even an objection against him, a question mark against his wisdom, a piece of unwisdom.—What? so all these great wise men were not only *décadents*, they were not even wise?—But I return to the problem of Socrates.

3

Socrates belonged by extraction to the lowest of the people: Socrates was rabble.* We know, we can even still see, how ugly he was.* But ugliness, in itself an objection, is to Greeks practically a refutation. Was Socrates actually really a Greek? Ugliness is often enough the expression of a cross-bred development *stunted* by cross-breeding. If not, then it appears as a development in *decline*. The anthropologists among criminologists tell us that the typical criminal is ugly: *monstrum in fronte, monstrum in animo.** But the criminal is a *décadent*. Was Socrates a typical criminal?—This would at least not be contradicted by that famous physiognomic judgement which sounded so rebarbative to Socrates' friends. When a foreigner who was an expert on faces came through Athens, he told Socrates to his face that he *was* a *monstrum*—that he was harbouring all the bad vices and desires. To which Socrates answered simply: 'You know me, sir!'*

4

Socrates' *décadence* is signalled not only by the avowed chaos and anarchy of his instincts: it is also signalled by the superfetation of the logical and that *jaundiced malice* which is his hallmark. Let us also not forget those auditory hallucinations which, as 'Socrates' Demon',* have taken on a religious interpretation. Everything about him is exaggerated, *buffo*, caricature; everything is at the same time concealed, ulteriorly motivated, subterranean. I am seeking to understand what was the idiosyncrasy* which gave rise to that Socratic equation, reason = virtue = happiness: that most bizarre of all equations which, in particular, has all the instincts of the older Hellene ranged against it.

5

With Socrates, Greek taste switches over in favour of dialectics: what is actually going on here? Above all it means a *noble* taste* is defeated; with dialectics the rabble comes out on top.* Before Socrates, dialectical manners were disapproved of in polite society: they were seen as bad manners because they were revealing.* The young were warned against them. People also mistrusted any such presentation of one's reasons. Respectable things, like respectable people, do not wear their reasons on their sleeves like that. It is indecent to show all five fingers. Anything which needs first to have itself proved is of little value. Wherever it is still good manners to be authoritative, and people do not 'justify' but command, the dialectician is a kind of buffoon: he is laughed at and not taken seriously.—Socrates was the buffoon who *got himself taken seriously*: what was actually going on here?

6

You choose dialectics only when you have no other means. You know that using it provokes mistrust, and that it is not very convincing. Nothing is easier to dismiss than the effect a dialectician produces: the experience of any assembly where speeches are made is proof of that. It can only be an *emergency defence* in the hands of those who have no other weapons left. You must need to *force* your being in the right out of people: otherwise you do not use it. That is why the Jews were dialecticians; Reynard the Fox* was one: what? and Socrates was one, too?—

7

—Is Socrates' irony an expression of revolt? of the rabble's resentment?* as one of the oppressed does he enjoy his own ferocity in the knife-thrusts of the syllogism? does he *avenge* himself on the noble men he fascinates?—As a dialectician you have a merciless tool in your hand; you can play the tyrant with it; you reveal by conquering. The dialectician leaves it to his opponent to prove he is not an idiot: he infuriates him and makes him helpless at the same time. The dialectician *disempowers* his opponent's intellect.—What? is dialectics just a form of *revenge* for Socrates?

8

I have indicated how Socrates could be repulsive: the fact that he *did* fascinate people needs all the more explaining.—For one thing he discovered a new kind of *agon** and was its first fencing master for the noble circles of Athens. He fascinated people by stirring up the agonal drive* of the Hellenes—he introduced a variation into the wrestling match between young men and youths. Socrates was also a great *eroticist*.

9

But Socrates sensed still more. He saw *behind* his noble Athenians; he realized that *his* case, his oddity of a case, was already unexceptional. The same kind of degenerescence was silently preparing itself every-where: old Athens was coming to an end.—And Socrates understood that the whole world *needed* him—his method, his cure, his personal trick of self-preservation... Everywhere the instincts were in an-archy; everywhere people were a few steps away from excess: the *monstrum in animo* was the general danger. 'The drives want to play the tyrant; we must invent a *counter-tyrant* who is stronger'... When that physiognomist had revealed to Socrates who he was—a den of all the bad desires—the great ironist said one more thing which gives the key to him. 'This is true,' he said, 'but I became master of all of them.' *How* did Socrates become master of *himself*? His was basically only the extreme case, only the most overt example of what was at that stage starting to become a general need: the fact that no one was master of himself any more,* that the instincts were turning *against* each other. He fascinated people by being this extreme case—his terrifying ugliness marked him out to every eye: it goes without saying that he exerted an even greater fascination as the answer, the solution, the apparent *cure* for this case.—

10

If it is necessary to make a tyrant out of *reason*, as Socrates did, then there must be no little danger that something else might play the tyrant. At that time people sensed in rationality a *deliverance*; neither Socrates nor his 'invalids' were free to be rational—it was *de rigueur*,* it was their *last* available means. The fanaticism with which the whole of Greek thought throws itself on rationality betrays a crisis: they were in danger, they had just *one* choice: either perish or—be *absurdly rational*... The moralism of Greek philosophers from Plato onwards is pathologically conditioned: likewise their appreciation of dialectics. Reason = virtue = happiness means simply: we must imitate Socrates and establish permanent *daylight* to combat the dark desires—the daylight of reason. We must be clever, clear, bright at all costs: any yielding to the instincts, to the unconscious,* leads *downwards*...

11

I have indicated how Socrates fascinated people: he appeared to be a physician, a saviour. Is it still necessary to demonstrate the error which lay in his belief in 'rationality at all costs'? It is a self-deception on the part of philosophers and moralists to believe that in waging war on *décadence* they are already emerging from it. It is beyond their power to emerge from it: whatever they choose as their means, their deliverance, is itself just another expression of *décadence*—they *alter* its expression, but they do not get rid of it. Socrates was a misunderstanding; *the entire morality of improvement,* Christianity's included, was a misunderstanding... The harshest daylight, rationality at all costs, life bright, cold, cautious, conscious, instinct-free, instinct-resistant: this itself was just an illness, a different illness—and definitely not a way back to 'virtue', 'health', happiness... To have to fight against the instincts— this is the formula for décadence: so long as life is ascendant, happiness equals instinct.—*

12

—Did he himself understand this, that cleverest* of all self-outwitters? Did he ultimately tell himself this, in the *wisdom* of his courage unto death?... Socrates *wanted* to die*—it was not Athens but *he* himself who administered the cup of poison; he forced Athens into it... 'Socrates is no physician,' he said quietly to himself: 'death alone is the physician here... Socrates himself has simply had a long illness...'

'REASON' IN PHILOSOPHY

1

You ask me what are all the idiosyncrasies of the philosophers? . . .
For one thing their lack of historical sense, their hatred of the very
idea of becoming,* their Egypticism. They think they are doing a
thing an *honour* when they dehistoricize it, *sub specie aeterni**—when
they make a mummy out of it. All that philosophers have been
handling for thousands of years is conceptual mummies; nothing
real has ever left their hands* alive. They kill things and stuff them,
these servants of conceptual idols, when they worship—they become
a mortal danger to everything when they worship. Death, change,
age, as well as procreation and growth, are objections—even refuta-
tions—for them. Whatever is, does not *become*; whatever becomes, *is*
not . . . Now they all believe, even to the point of desperation, in
being.* But because they cannot gain possession of it they look for
reasons as to why it is being withheld from them. 'There must be
some pretence, some deception going on, preventing us from per-
ceiving being: where's the deceiver hiding?'—'We've got him', they
cry in rapturous delight, 'it's our sensuousness! These senses, *which
are otherwise so immoral, too*, they are deceiving us about the *real*
world.* Moral: free yourself from sense-deception, from becoming,
history, lies—history is nothing but belief in the senses, belief in lies.
Moral: say no to anything which believes in the senses, to the whole
of the rest of humanity: they are all just "the populace". Be a philosopher, be a mummy, represent monotono-theism by miming a
gravedigger!—And above all away with the *body*, this pitiful *idée
fixe* of the senses! afflicted with every logical error there is, refuted,
even impossible, though it is cheeky enough to act as if it were
real!' . . .

2

I shall set apart, with great respect, the name of *Heraclitus*.* If the
rest of the philosophical populace rejected the evidence of the senses
because they showed multiplicity and change, he rejected their

evidence because they showed things as if they had duration and unity. Heraclitus, too, did the senses an injustice. They do not lie either in the way that the Eleatics* believe, or as he believed—they do not lie at all. What we *make* of their evidence is what gives rise to the lie, for example the lie of unity, the lie of materiality, of substance, of duration . . . 'Reason' is what causes us to falsify the evidence of the senses. If the senses show becoming, passing away, change, they do not lie . . . But Heraclitus will always be right that Being is an empty fiction. The 'apparent' world is the only one: the 'real world' has just been *lied on* . . .

3

—And what fine instruments of observation we have in our senses! This nose, for example, of which not one philosopher has yet spoken in reverence and gratitude, is nevertheless actually the most delicate instrument we have at our command: it can register minimal differences in movement which even the spectroscope fails to register. We possess science nowadays precisely to the extent that we decided to *accept* the evidence of the senses—when we were still learning to sharpen them, arm them, think them through to the end. The rest is abortion and not-yet-science: to wit, metaphysics, theology, psychology, theory of knowledge. *Or* the science of forms, the theory of signs: like logic and that applied logic, mathematics. Reality is nowhere to be found in them, not even as a problem; nor does the question arise as to what actual value a sign-convention like logic has.—

4

The *other* idiosyncrasy of the philosophers is no less dangerous: it consists in mistaking the last for the first.* They put what comes at the end—unfortunately! for it should not come anywhere!—the 'highest concepts', i.e. the most general, emptiest concepts, the last wisp of evaporating reality, at the beginning *as* the beginning. This is once again simply the expression of their kind of reverence: the higher *is not allowed* to grow out of the lower, *is not allowed* to have grown at all . . . Moral: everything first-rate must be *causa sui*.* If it is descended from something else, this is seen as an objection and brings its value into question. All the supreme values are first-rate; all the highest concepts—being, the absolute, the good, the true, the perfect—none of them can have become, so they *must* be *causa sui*. Equally, though, none of them can differ from the others or conflict with them ... Hence their astounding notion of 'God' ... The last, thinnest, emptiest, is put first, as cause in itself, as *ens realissimum** ... Oh that humanity had to take seriously the brain-feverish fantasies spun out by the sick!*—And it has paid dearly for it! ...

5

—Let us finally set against this the different way in which *we* (—I say we out of politeness ...) contemplate the problem of error and appearance. In former times people took alteration, change, becoming in general as proof of appearance, as a sign that there must be something there leading us astray. Nowadays, conversely—and precisely in so far as the prejudice called 'reason' compels us to establish unity, identity, duration, substance, cause, materiality, Being—we see ourselves to a certain extent tangled up in error, *forced* into error; as sure as we are, on the basis of stringent checking, *that* the error is here. It is no different from the movements of the great stars: in their case error has our eye as its constant advocate, here it has our *language*. Language is assigned by its emergence to the time of the most rudimentary form of psychology: we become involved in a crude fetishism when we make ourselves conscious of the basic premisses of the metaphysics of language, in plain words: of *reason*. *This* is what sees doer and deed everywhere: it believes in the will as cause in general; it believes in the 'I',* in the I as Being, in the I as substance, and *projects* the belief in the I-substance onto all things— only then does it *create* the concept 'thing' ... Being is thought in, *foisted in* everywhere as cause; only following on from the conception 'I' is the concept 'Being' derived ... At the beginning stands the great disaster of an error that the will is something *at work*—that will is a *capacity* ... Nowadays we know that it is just a word ... Very much later, in a world a thousand times more enlightened, philosophers were surprised to realize how *assured*, how subjectively *certain* they were in handling the categories of reason*—which, they concluded, could not come from the empirical world, since the empirical world stands in contradiction to them. *So where do they come from?*—And in

India as in Greece* they made the same mistake: 'we must once have been at home in a higher world (—instead of *in a very much lower one*: which would have been the truth!), we must have been divine *because* we have reason!' . . . In fact nothing has had a more naïve power of persuasion so far than the error of Being, as formulated, for example, by the Eleatics: for it has on its side every word, every sentence we speak!—Even the opponents of the Eleatics still succumbed to the seduction of their concept of Being: among others Democritus,* when he invented his *atom* . . . 'Reason' in language: oh what a deceitful old woman!* I am afraid we are not getting rid of God because we still believe in grammar . . .

6

People will be grateful to me for condensing such an essential new insight into four theses: this way I am easing comprehension; this way I am inviting contradiction.

First Proposition. The reasons which have been given for designating 'this' world as apparent actually account for its reality—any *other* kind of reality is absolutely unprovable.

Second Proposition. The characteristics which have been given to the 'true Being' of things are the characteristics of non-Being, of *nothingness*—the 'real world' has been constructed from the contradiction of the actual world: an apparent world, indeed, to the extent that it is merely a *moral-optical* illusion.

Third Proposition. Concocting stories* about a world 'other' than this one is utterly senseless, unless we have within us a powerful instinct to slander, belittle, cast suspicion on life: in which case we are *avenging* ourselves on life with the phantasmagoria of 'another', 'better' life.

Fourth Proposition. Dividing the world into a 'real' one and an 'apparent' one, whether in the manner of Christianity, or of Kant* (a *crafty* Christian, when all's said and done), is but a suggestion of *décadence*—a symptom of *declining* life . . . The fact that the artist values appearance more highly than reality is no objection to this proposition. For 'appearance' here means reality *once more*, only selected, strengthened, corrected . . . The tragic artist is *no* pessimist—on the contrary, he says *yes* to all that is questionable and even terrible; he is *Dionysian**. . .

HOW THE 'REAL WORLD' FINALLY BECAME A FABLE

History* of an Error

1. The real world attainable for the wise man, the pious man, the virtuous man—he lives in it, *he is it*.

(Most ancient form of the idea, relatively clever, simple, convincing. Paraphrase of the proposition: 'I, Plato, *am* the truth.')

2. The real world unattainable for now, but promised to the wise man, the pious man, the virtuous man ('to the sinner who repents').

(Progress of the idea: it becomes more cunning, more insidious, more incomprehensible*—*it becomes a woman*,* it becomes Christian . . .)

3. The real world unattainable, unprovable, unpromisable, but the mere thought of it a consolation, an obligation, an imperative.

(The old sun in the background, but seen through mist and scepticism; the idea become sublime, pale, Nordic, Königsbergian.)*

4. The real world—unattainable? At any rate unattained. And since unattained also *unknown*. Hence no consolation, redemption, obligation either: what could something unknown oblige us to do? . . .

(Break of day. First yawn of reason. Cock-crow of positivism.)*

5. The 'real world'—an idea with no further use, no longer even an obligation—an idea become useless, superfluous, *therefore* a refuted idea: let us do away with it!

(Broad daylight; breakfast; return of *bon sens** and cheerfulness; Plato's shameful blush; din from all free spirits.)*

6. The real world—we have done away with it: what world was left? the apparent one, perhaps? . . . But no! *with the real world we have also done away with the apparent one!*

(Noon; moment of the shortest shadow; end of the longest error; pinnacle of humanity; INCIPIT ZARATHUSTRA.)*

MORALITY AS ANTI-NATURE*

I

All passions have a period in which they are merely fateful, in which they draw their victims down by weight of stupidity—and a later, very much later one, in which they marry the spirit, 'spiritualize' themselves. In former times, because of the stupidity of passion, people waged war on passion itself: they plotted to destroy it—all the old moral monsters are in complete agreement that 'il faut tuer les passions'.* The most famous formula for this can be found in the New Testament, in that Sermon on the Mount where, incidentally, things are by no means viewed *from on high*. Here it is said, for example, with reference to sexuality, 'if thine eye offend thee, pluck it out':* fortunately no Christian acts according to this precept. *Destroying* the passions and desires merely in order to avoid their stupidity and the disagreeable consequences of their stupidity seems to us nowadays to be itself simply an acute form of stupidity. We no longer marvel at dentists who *pull out* teeth to stop them hurting... On the other hand, to be fair, it should be admitted that there was no way in which, on the soil* from which Christianity grew up, the concept of '*spiritualization* of passion' could even be conceived. For the first church, as is well known, fought *against* the 'intelligent' on the side of the 'poor in spirit':* how could one expect from it an intelligent war on passion?—The church fights against passion with every kind of excision: its method, its 'cure', is *castratism*. It never asks 'how does one spiritualize, beautify, deify a desire?'—in disciplining, it has put the emphasis throughout the ages on eradication (of sensuality, pride, the urge to rule, to possess, to avenge).—But attacking the passions at the root means attacking life at the root: the practice of the church is *inimical to life*...

2

The same means—castration, eradication—are instinctively chosen by those fighting against a desire who are too weak-willed, too degenerate to be able to set themselves a measure in it: by those types who need La Trappe,* metaphorically speaking (and non-metaphorically—), some definitive declaration of enmity, a *gulf* between themselves and a passion. Only the degenerate find radical means indispensable; weakness of will, more specifically the inability *not* to react to a stimulus,* is itself simply another form of degenerescence. Radical enmity, mortal enmity against sensuality, remains a thought-provoking symptom: it justifies you in speculating about the overall condition of such an excessive.—This enmity, this hatred reaches its peak, moreover, only when such types are no longer steadfast enough even for a radical cure, for renouncing their 'devil'. If you survey the whole history of priests and philosophers, and artists, too: it is *not* the impotent who have said the most poisonous things against the senses; *nor* is it the ascetics, but the impossible ascetics, those who could have done with being ascetics* ...

3

The spiritualization of sensuality is called *love*: it is a great triumph over Christianity. A further triumph is our spiritualization of *enmity*. This consists in our profound understanding of the value of having enemies: in short, our doing and deciding the converse of what people previously thought and decided. Throughout the ages the church has wanted to destroy its enemies: we, we immoralists and anti-Christians, see it as to our advantage that the church exists ... Even in the field of politics enmity has nowadays become more spiritual—much cleverer, much more thoughtful, much *gentler*. Almost every party sees that its interest in self-preservation is best served if its opposite number does not lose its powers; the same is true of great politics.* A new creation in particular, such as the new Reich, needs enemies more than it does friends: only by being opposed does it feel necessary; only by being opposed does it *become* necessary ... Our behaviour towards our 'inner enemy' is no different: here, too, we have spiritualized enmity; here, too, we have grasped its *value*. One is *fruitful* only at the price of being rich in opposites; one stays *young* only on condition that the soul does not have a stretch and desire peace ... Nothing has become more alien to us than that desideratum of old, 'peace of soul', the *Christian* desideratum; nothing makes us less envious than ruminant morality and the luxuriant happiness of a good conscience. Renouncing war means renouncing *great* life ... In many cases, of course, 'peace of soul' is simply a misunderstanding—something *else* which is just unable to give itself a more honest name. Without digression or prejudice, a few cases. 'Peace of soul' can be, for example, a rich animality radiating gently out into the moral (or religious) domain. Or the onset of tiredness, the first shadow which evening, any kind of evening, casts. Or a sign that the air is moist, that southerly winds are drawing close. Or unwitting gratitude for successful digestion (sometimes called 'love of humanity'). Or the falling quiet of a convalescent as he finds everything tastes good again and waits ... Or the state which follows the powerful satisfaction of our ruling passion, the sense of well-being at being uncommonly sated. Or the infirmity of our will, our desires, our vices. Or laziness persuaded by vanity to dress itself up in moral garb. Or the advent of certainty, even terrible certainty, after a long period of tension and torment at the hands of uncertainty. Or the expression of maturity and mastery in the midst of doing, creating, affecting, willing; breathing easily, 'freedom of the will'* *achieved* ... *Twilight of the idols*: who knows? perhaps also just a kind of 'peace of soul' ...

4

—I shall make a principle into a formula. All naturalism in morality, i.e. every *healthy* morality, is governed by a vital instinct—one or other of life's decrees is fulfilled through a specific canon of 'shalls' and 'shall nots', one or other of the obstructions and hostilities on life's way is thus removed. *Anti-natural* morality, i.e. almost every morality which has hitherto been taught, revered, and preached, turns on the contrary precisely *against* the vital instincts—it is at times secret, at times loud and brazen in *condemning* these instincts. In saying 'God looks at the heart'* it says no to the lowest and highest of life's desires, and takes God to be an *enemy of life* ... The saint, in whom God is well pleased,* is the ideal castrato ... Life ends where the 'kingdom of God' *begins* ...

5

Once you have grasped the heinousness of such a revolt against life, which has become almost sacrosanct in Christian morality, then fortunately you have also grasped something else: the futile, feigned, absurd, *lying* nature of such a revolt. A condemnation of life on the part of the living remains in the last resort merely the symptom of a specific kind of life: the question as to whether it is justifiable or not simply does not arise. You would need to be situated *outside* life, and at the same time to know life as well as someone—many people, everyone—who has lived it, to be allowed even to touch on the problem of the *value* of life: reason enough for realizing that the problem is an inaccessible problem to us. Whenever we speak of values, we speak under the inspiration—from the perspective—of life: life itself forces us to establish values; life itself evaluates through us *when* we posit values ... It follows from this that even that *anti-nature of a morality* which conceives of God as the antithesis and condemnation of life is merely a value judgement on the part of life— *which* life? *what* kind of life?—But I have already given the answer: declining, weakened, tired, condemned life. Morality as it has hitherto been understood—and formulated by Schopenhauer, lastly, as 'denial of the will to life'*—is the *décadence instinct* itself making an imperative out of itself: it says: '*perish!*'—it is the judgement of the condemned ...

6

Let us finally consider what naïvety it is in general to say 'man *should* be such and such!' Reality shows us a delightful abundance of types, the richness that comes from an extravagant play and alternation of forms: to which some wretched loafer of a moralist says: 'no! man should be *different*'? ... He even knows how man should be, this maundering miseryguts: he paints himself on the wall and says '*ecce homo!*'* ... But even when the moralist turns just to the individual and says to him: '*you* should be such and such!' he does not stop making a fool of himself. The individual is a piece of fate from top to bottom, one more law, one more necessity for all that is to come and will be. Telling him to change means demanding that everything should change, even backwards ... And indeed there have been consistent moralists who wanted man to be different, namely virtuous; they wanted him to be in their image,* namely a miseryguts: to which end they *denied* the world! No minor madness! No modest kind of immodesty! ... Morality, in so far as it *condemns*—in itself, and *not* in

view of life's concerns, considerations, intentions*—is a specific
error on which we should not take pity, a *degenerate's idiosyncrasy*
which has wrought untold damage!... We who are different, we
immoralists, on the contrary, have opened our hearts to all kinds of
understanding, comprehending, *approving*. We do not readily deny;
we seek our honour in being *affirmative*.* More and more our eyes
have been opened to that economy* which still needs and can exploit
all that is rejected by the holy madness of the priest, of the priest's *sick*
reason; to that economy in the law of life which can gain advantage
even from the repulsive species of the miseryguts, the priest, the
virtuous man—*what* advantage?—But we ourselves, we immoralists
are the answer here...

THE FOUR GREAT ERRORS

I

Error of Confusing Cause and Consequence.—There is no error more dangerous than that of confusing the *consequence with the cause*: I call it the real ruination of reason. Nevertheless this error is among the most long-standing and recent of humanity's habits: it is even sanctified by us, and bears the name 'religion', 'morality'. *Every* proposition which religion and morality formulate contains it; priests and moral legislators are the originators of this ruination of reason.—I shall take one example: everyone knows the book by the famous Cornaro,* in which he recommends his meagre diet as a recipe for a long and happy life—and a virtuous one, too. Few books have been read so much; even now in England many thousands of copies of it are printed annually. I have no doubt that hardly any book (with due exception for the Bible) has done as much damage, *shortened* as many lives as this well-intentioned *curiosum*. The reason: confusion of the consequence with the cause. The worthy Italian gentleman saw in his diet the *cause* of his long life: whereas the precondition for a long life—extraordinarily slow metabolism, low consumption—was the cause of his meagre diet. He was not free to eat a little *or* a lot; his frugality was *not* an act of 'free will': he fell ill if he ate any more. But anyone who is not a carp* finds it not only good but necessary to eat *properly*. A scholar in *our* day, with his rapid consumption of nervous energy, would destroy himself on Cornaro's regimen. *Crede experto.**—

2

The most general formula underlying every religion and morality is: 'Do this and that, stop this and that—then you will be happy! Or else . . .' Every morality, every religion *is* this imperative—I call it the great original sin of reason, *immortal unreason*. In my mouth that formula is transformed into its inversion—*first* example of my 'revaluation of all values': a well-balanced person, a 'happy man', *has* to do certain actions and instinctively shies away from others; he carries over the order which his physiology represents into his relations with people and things. In a formula: his virtue is the *consequence* of his happiness ... A long life, numerous progeny, are *not* the reward for virtue; instead, virtue is itself that slowing down of the metabolism which among other things also brings a long life, numerous progeny, in short *Cornarism* in its wake.—The church and morality say: 'a race, a people is destroyed by vice and extravagance.' My *restored* reason says: if a people is destroyed, if it physiologically degenerates, then this is *followed* by vice and extravagance (i.e. the need for ever stronger and more frequent stimuli, familiar to every exhausted type). This young man grows prematurely pale and listless. His friends say: such and such an illness is to blame. I say: *the fact that* he fell ill, *the fact that* he could not withstand the illness, was already the consequence of an impoverished life, of hereditary exhaustion. The newspaper reader says: this party will destroy itself by such a mistake. My *higher* politics says: a party which makes such mistakes is already finished—its instinct is no longer sure. Every mistake, in every sense, results from a degeneration of instinct, a disgregation of the will—which is almost a definition of the *bad*. Everything *good* is instinct—and therefore easy, necessary, free. Effort is an objection; a god is typologically different from a hero (in my language: *light* feet* the foremost attribute of divinity).

3

Error of a False Causality.—People throughout the ages have believed they knew what a cause is: but where did we get our knowledge, more precisely our belief that we know? From the realm of the celebrated 'inner facts', not one of which has so far turned out to be real. We believed that we ourselves, in the act of willing, were causes; we thought that we were at least catching causality there *in the act*. Likewise people were in no doubt that all the *antecedentia* of an action, its causes, were to be sought in consciousness and would be rediscovered there if sought—as 'motives': otherwise they would not have been free *to do* it, responsible *for* it. Finally, who would have denied that a thought is caused? that the 'I' causes the thought? ... Of these three 'inner facts', by which causality seemed to be authenticated, the first and most convincing one is that of the *will as cause*; the conception of a consciousness ('mind') as cause and, later still, of the 'I' (the 'subject') as cause came only afterwards, once the causality of the will had been established as given, as *empirical*... Since then we have thought better of all this. Nowadays we no longer believe a word of it. The 'inner world' is full of illusions and jack-o'-lanterns: the will is one of them. The will no longer moves anything, and therefore no longer explains anything either—it simply accompanies events, and can even be absent. The so-called 'motive': another error. Merely a surface phenomenon of consciousness, an accessory to the act, which does more to conceal the *antecedentia* of an act than to represent them. And as for the I! It has become a fable, a fiction, a play on words: it has completely given up thinking, feeling, and willing!... What is the result? There are no mental causes at all! All the apparently empirical evidence for them has gone to the devil! *That* is the result!—And we had subjected this 'empirical evidence' to a pretty piece of abuse; we had *created* the world on the basis of it as a world of causes, a world of will, a spirit world*... The most ancient and long-established psychology was at work here, and it did absolutely nothing else: in its eyes every event was an action, every action the result of a will; in its eyes the world became a multiplicity of agents, an agent (a 'subject') foisting itself onto every event. Man's three 'inner facts', the things he believed in most firmly—the will, the mind, the I—were projected out of himself: he derived the concept of Being from the concept of the I, and posited the existence of 'things' after his own image, after his concept of the I as cause. No wonder if, later on, he only ever rediscovered in things *what he had put in them*.—The thing itself, to say it again, the concept of thing: just a reflection of the belief in the I as cause... And even your atom, my dear mechanicians and physicists, how much error, how much rudimentary psychology still remains in your atom! Not to speak of the 'thing in itself',* the *horrendum pudendum** of the metaphysicians! The error of confusing the mind as cause with reality! And made the measure of reality! And called *God*!—

4

Error of Imaginary Causes.—To take dreams as my starting point:* a specific sensation, for example one which results from a distant cannon-shot, has a cause foisted onto it after the event* (often a complete little novel, in which the dreamer himself is the main character). Meanwhile the sensation persists, in a kind of resonance: it is as if it waits for the causal drive to allow it to step into the foreground—now no longer as chance, but as 'meaning'. The cannon-shot makes its appearance in a *causal* way, in an apparent reversal of time. The later thing, the motivation, is experienced first, often together with a hundred details which pass by like lightning, and the shot follows... What has happened? The ideas which a certain state *generated* have been mistakenly understood as its cause.—In fact we do the same thing in waking life. Most of our general feelings—every kind of inhibition, pressure, excitation, explosion in the play and counter-play of the organs, such as the state of the *nervus sympathicus** in particular—stimulate our causal drive: we want a *reason* for having *such and such* a feeling, for feeling bad or feeling good. We are never satisfied with simply establishing the fact *that* we have such and such a feeling: we license this fact—become *conscious* of it—only *when* we have given it a kind of motivation.—Memory, which in such cases comes into operation without our knowledge, fetches up earlier, similar states and the causal interpretations entwined with them—*not* their causality. Of course the belief that the ideas, the concomitant processes in consciousness, were the causes, is fetched up by memory, too. Thus we become *used* to a specific causal interpretation which, in truth, inhibits any *inquiry* into causes and even rules it out.

5

Psychological Explanation for This.—Tracing something unknown back to something known gives relief, soothes, satisfies, and furthermore gives a feeling of power. The unknown brings with it danger, disquiet, worry—one's first instinct is to *get rid of* these awkward conditions. First principle: any explanation is better than none. Because it is basically just a question of wanting to get rid of oppressive ideas, we are not exactly strict with the means we employ to get rid of them: the first idea which can explain the unknown as known feels so good that it is 'held to be true'. Proof of *pleasure* ('strength') as criterion of truth.—The causal drive is therefore determined and stimulated by the feeling of fear. The 'why?' is intended, if at all possible, not so much to yield the cause in its own right as rather a *kind of cause*—a soothing, liberating, relief-giving cause. The fact that something already *known*, experienced, inscribed in the memory is established as a cause, is the first consequence of this need. The new, the unexperienced, the alien is ruled out as a cause. So it is not just a kind of explanation which is sought as cause, but a *select* and *privileged* kind of explanation, the kind which has allowed the feeling of the alien, new, unexperienced to be dispelled most quickly and most often—the *most usual* explanations.—Result: one way of positing causes becomes increasingly prevalent, is concentrated into a system and ultimately emerges as *dominant*, i.e. simply ruling out *other* causes and explanations.—The banker's first thoughts are of 'business', the Christian's of 'sin', the girl's of her love.

6

The Entire Realm of Morality and Religion Belongs Under This Concept of Imaginary Causes.—'Explanation' for *unpleasant* general feelings. They are determined by beings which are hostile to us (evil spirits: most famous case—misunderstanding of hysterics as witches). They are determined by actions which cannot be sanctioned (the feeling of 'sin', of 'sinfulness', foisted onto a physiological unease—one can always find reasons to be dissatisfied with oneself). They are determined as punishments, as a repayment for something we should not have done, should not have *been* (impudently generalized by Schopenhauer into a proposition which reveals morality as it really is, as the poisoner and slanderer of life: 'Every great pain, whether bodily or mental, states what we deserve; for it could not come to us if we did not deserve it'—*World as Will and Representation*).* They are determined as the consequences of thoughtless actions which turned out badly (—the emotions, the senses posited as cause, as 'to blame'; physiological crises interpreted with the help of *other* crises as 'deserved').—'Explanation' for *pleasant* general feelings. These are determined by trust in God. They are determined by the awareness of good works (the so-called 'good conscience', a physiological state which sometimes looks so similar to successful digestion that one could confuse the two). They are determined by the successful outcome of undertakings (—naïvely false conclusion: the successful outcome of an undertaking gives a hypochondriac or a Pascal* no pleasant general feelings at all). They are determined by faith,

charity, hope—the Christian virtues.*—In truth all these so-called
explanations are states which *result* from something, a kind of translation of feelings of pleasure or displeasure into the wrong dialect: one
is in a position to hope *because* one's basic physiological feeling is
strong and rich again; one trusts in God *because* one is calmed by a
feeling of plenitude and strength.—Morality and religion belong
entirely under the *psychology of error*: in every single case cause and
effect are confused; or truth is confused with the effect of what is
believed to be true; or a state of consciousness is confused with the
causality of this state.

7

Error of Free Will.—We no longer have any sympathy nowadays for
the concept 'free will': we know only too well what it is—the most
disreputable piece of trickery the theologians have produced, aimed
at making humanity 'responsible' in their sense, i.e. at *making it
dependent on them* . . . I shall give here simply the psychology behind
every kind of making people responsible.—Wherever responsibilities
are sought, it is usually the instinct for *wanting to punish and judge* that
is doing the searching. Becoming is stripped of its innocence* once
any state of affairs is traced back to a will, to intentions, to responsible
acts: the doctrine of the will was fabricated essentially for the purpose
of punishment, i.e. of *wanting to find guilty*. The old psychology as a
whole, the psychology of the will, presupposes the fact that its
originators, the priests at the head of ancient communities, wanted
to give themselves the *right* to impose punishments—or give God the
right to do so . . . People were thought of as 'free' so that they could be
judged and punished—so that they could become *guilty*:* consequently every action *had* to be thought of as willed, the origin of
every action as located in consciousness (—thus the *most fundamental*
piece of counterfeiting *in psychologicis** became the principle of
psychology itself). Nowadays, since we are engaged in a movement
in the *opposite* direction, since we immoralists especially are seeking
with all our strength to eliminate the concepts of guilt and punishment again and to cleanse psychology, history, nature, social institutions and sanctions of them, there is in our view no more radical
opposition than that which comes from the theologians who, with
their concept of the 'moral world order', persist in plaguing the

innocence of becoming with 'punishment' and 'guilt'. Christianity is
a metaphysics of the hangman . . .

8

What can *our* doctrine be, though?—That no one *gives* man his
qualities, neither God, nor society, nor his parents and ancestors,
nor *man himself* (—the nonsense of the last idea rejected here was
taught as 'intelligible freedom'* by Kant, perhaps already by Plato,*
too). *No one* is responsible for simply being there, for being made in
such and such a way, for existing under such conditions, in such
surroundings. The fatality of one's being cannot be derived from the
fatality of all that was and will be. *No one* is the result of his own
intention, his own will, his own purpose; *no one* is part of an experiment to achieve an 'ideal person' or an 'ideal of happiness' or an 'ideal
of morality'—it is absurd to want to *discharge* one's being onto some
purpose or other. *We* invented the concept 'purpose': in reality,
'purpose' is *absent* . . . One is necessary, one is a piece of fate, one
belongs to the whole, one *is* in the whole—there is nothing which
could judge, measure, compare, condemn our Being, for that would
mean judging, measuring, comparing, condemning the whole . . . *But
there is nothing apart from the whole!* That no one is made responsible
any more, that a kind of Being cannot be traced back to a *causa
prima*,* that the world is no unity, either as sensorium or as 'mind',
this alone is the great liberation—this alone re-establishes the *innocence*
of becoming . . . The concept 'God' has been the greatest *objection* to
existence so far . . . We deny God, we deny responsibility in God: *this*
alone is how we redeem the world.—

THE 'IMPROVERS' OF HUMANITY

I

People are familiar with my call for the philosopher to place himself *beyond* good and evil*—to have the illusion of moral judgement *beneath* him. This call results from an insight which I was the first to formulate:* *that there are no moral facts at all.* Moral judgement has this in common with religious judgement, that it believes in realities which do not exist. Morality is merely an interpretation of certain phenomena, more precisely a *mis*interpretation. Moral judgement pertains, like religious judgement, to a level of ignorance on which the very concept of the real, the distinction between the real and the imaginary, is still lacking: so that 'truth', on such a level, designates nothing but what we nowadays call 'illusions'. In this respect moral judgement should never be taken literally: as such it is only ever an absurdity. But as a *semiotics** it remains inestimable: it reveals, at least to anyone who knows, the most valuable realities of cultures and interiorities which did not *know* enough to 'understand' themselves. Morality is merely sign language, merely symptomatology: you must already know *what* is going on in order to profit by it.

2

A first, quite provisional example. Throughout the ages people have wanted to 'improve' humanity: this above all is what has been called morality. But under the same word the most extraordinary variety of tendencies is hiding. Both the *taming* of the beast man and the *breeding* of a particular species of man have been called 'improvement': these zoological terms alone express realities—realities, of course, about which the typical 'improver', the priest, knows nothing—*wants* to know nothing . . . To call the taming of an animal its 'improvement' is to our ears almost a joke. Anyone who knows what goes on in menageries will doubt that a beast is 'improved' there. It is weakened, it is made less harmful, it is turned into a *diseased* beast through the depressive emotion of fear, through pain, through wounding, through hunger.—It is no different with the tamed human being whom the priest has 'improved'. In the early Middle Ages, when the church was in fact primarily a menagerie, people on all sides hunted down the finest examples of the 'blond beast'*—they 'improved' the noble Teutons, for example. But afterwards what did such an 'improved' Teuton look like, once he had been tempted into the monastery? Like a caricature of a human being, like an abortion: he had become a 'sinner', he was stuck in a cage, he had been locked in between nothing but dreadful concepts . . . There he now lay, sick, wretched, malevolent towards himself; filled with hatred of the vital drives, filled with suspicion towards all that was still strong and happy. In short, a 'Christian' . . . Physiologically speaking: in the struggle with the beast, making it sick is the only *possible* means of weakening it. The church understood this: it *ruined* man, it weakened him—but it claimed to have 'improved' him . . .

3

Let us take the other case of so-called morality, the case of *breeding* a particular race and kind. The most magnificent example of this is provided by Indian morality, sanctioned as a religion in the *Law of Manu*.* Here the task is set of breeding no fewer than four races at once: a priestly one, a warrior one, a commercial and agricultural one, and finally a servant race, the Sudras. Clearly we are no longer among animal-tamers here: a kind of human being which is a hundred times milder and more rational is required in order just to conceive such a breeding plan. One breathes a sigh of relief on emerging from the sickly dungeon-air of Christianity into this healthier, higher, *wider* world. How miserable the 'New Testament' is compared to Manu, how badly it smells!—But even this organization needed to be *ter- rible*—this time in struggling not with the beast, but with *its* anti- thetical concept, the unbred human being, mish-mash man, the Chandala.* And again it had no other way of making him harmless and weak than by making him *sick*—it was a struggle with the 'great number'. There is perhaps nothing which contradicts our sensibility more than *these* defensive measures of Indian morality. The third edict, for example (*Avadana-Shastra* I), 'Of the Unclean Vegetables', decrees that the only sustenance the Chandala should be allowed is garlic and onions, given that the holy scripture forbids anyone to give them grain, or fruits which contain seeds, or *water*, or fire. The same edict lays down that the water they need may not be drawn from either the rivers or the springs or the pools, but only from the approaches to swamps and from holes formed by the footprints of animals. Similarly they are forbidden to wash their laundry or *to wash themselves*, since the water they are mercifully granted may only be used to quench their thirst. Lastly a ban on Sudra women assisting Chandala women in giving birth, another similar one on the latter *assisting each other* . . . The success of such sanitary policing was not slow in coming: murderous plagues, dreadful venereal diseases, and on top of that 'the law of the knife', decreeing circumcision for the male children and the removal of the *labia minora* for the female ones.—Manu himself says: 'the Chandala are the fruit of adultery, incest, and crime [—this the *necessary* consequence of the concept of breeding]. For clothes they shall have only the rags from corpses, for dishes broken pots, for jewellery old iron, for divine service only the evil spirits; they shall roam without repose from one place to another. They are forbidden to write from left to right or to use their right hand for writing: the use of the right hand and of writing from left to right is reserved for the *virtuous ones* alone, the people of *pedigree*.'—

4

These ordinances are instructive enough: we have in them *Aryan* humaneness perfectly pure, perfectly original—we learn that the concept of 'pure blood' is the opposite of a harmless notion. On the other hand it becomes clear *which* is the people in which the hatred, the Chandala-hatred of this 'humaneness' has been perpetuated, has become a religion, has become *genius* . . . From this point of view the gospels are a document of the first order; even more so the Book of Enoch.*—Christianity, rooted in Judaism and only understandable as having grown from this soil, represents the *counter-movement* to any morality of breeding, of pedigree, of privilege—it is the *anti-Aryan* religion *par excellence*: Christianity is the revaluation of all Aryan values, the triumph of Chandala values, the gospel preached to the poor and the lowly,* the total revolt of everything downtrodden, miserable, ill-begotten, botched, against 'pedigree'*—the immortal revenge of the Chandala as *religion of love* . . .

5

The morality of *breeding* and the morality of *taming* are altogether worthy of each other in the ways they win through: we can set it down as our highest proposition that in order to *make* morality one must have an absolute will to its opposite. This is the great *uncanny* problem which I have been investigating the longest: the psychology of the 'improvers' of humanity. A little and fundamentally modest fact, the so-called *pia fraus*,* first gave me access to this problem: the *pia fraus*, the legacy of all the philosophers and priests who have 'improved' humanity. Neither Manu nor Plato nor Confucius,* nor the Jewish and Christian doctors, have ever doubted their *right* to lie. Nor have they doubted *quite different rights*... Expressing it in a formula, one might say: *all* the means by which humanity was meant to have been made moral so far were fundamentally *immoral*.—

WHAT THE GERMANS LACK

I

Among Germans it is not enough these days to have a spirited mind: you have to take it as well, to *seize* such spirit . . .

Perhaps I know the Germans; perhaps I can tell even them a few truths. The new Germany* represents a great quantity of inherited and acquired ability, so that for a time it can expend—even squander—its accumulated wealth of energy. It is *not* a high culture that has assumed mastery with it, still less a delicate taste, a noble 'beauty' of the instincts; but *more manly* virtues than any other country in Europe has to show for itself. Much good cheer and self-respect, much assuredness in its dealings, in reciprocating its obligations, much industriousness, much tenacity—and an inherited sense of moderation which is more in need of the goad than the brake shoe. I would add that people here still obey without being humiliated by obedience . . . And no one despises his opponent . . .

One can tell that it is my wish to be fair to the Germans: I would not want to be untrue to myself in doing so—I must therefore also raise my objection to them. You pay a high price for coming to power: power *stultifies* . . . The Germans—they used once to be called the nation of thinkers:* do they still think at all nowadays?—The Germans now are bored with the mind, the Germans now distrust the mind; politics swallows up all their ability to take really intellectual things seriously—'Deutschland, Deutschland über Alles',* I am afraid that was the end of German philosophy . . . 'Are there any German philosophers? are there any German poets? are there any *good* German books?' people ask me when I am abroad. I blush, but with the bravery which is mine even in desperate situations, I answer: 'Yes, *Bismarck!*'*—Should I also just confess which books people read these days? . . . Cursed instinct of mediocrity!—

2

—What the German mind *could* be—who might not already have had his melancholy thoughts on that question! But this nation has made

itself stupid on purpose, for practically a millennium: nowhere have
the two great European narcotics, alcohol and Christianity,* been
abused with greater depravity. Recently even a third has been added,
which on its own can dispatch any fine and daring agility of the mind:
music, our constipated, constipating German music.*—How much
tiresome heaviness, lameness, dampness, night-gown,* how much
beer there is in the German intellect! How is it actually possible for
young men who devote their existence to the most intellectual of
goals not to feel in themselves the first instinct of intellectuality, *the
mind's instinct for self-preservation*—and to drink beer? . . . The alco-
holism of young scholars may not be a question mark over their
erudition—you can be even a great scholar* without a mind—but
in every other respect it remains a problem.—Where would you not
find that delicate degeneration which beer produces in the mind!
Once, in a case which almost became famous, I put my finger on such
a degeneration—the degeneration of our foremost German freethinker, *clever* David Strauss,* into the author of a barstool-gospel
and 'new faith' . . . Not for nothing had he pledged himself to his
'brown beloved' in verse*—faithful unto death . . .

3

—I was speaking about the German mind, saying that it is getting
coarser, that it is becoming shallow. Is that enough?—It is basically
something quite different which alarms me: the way German seriousness, German profundity, German *passion* in intellectual matters is
going more and more downhill. It is the pathos that has changed, not
just the intellectual complexion.—I come into contact here and there
with German universities:* what an atmosphere prevails among the
scholars there, what an arid, undemanding, insipid intellectuality! It
would be a profound misunderstanding if anyone tried to raise an
objection to me here in German science*—and furthermore proof
that they had not read a single word of mine. For seventeen years* I
have not tired of highlighting the *de-intellectualizing* influence of our
present-day scientific practice. The hard life of helotry to which the
immense range of the sciences nowadays condemns every individual
is one of the main reasons why fuller, richer, *deeper*-natured types can
no longer find any education *or educators*atisfy suited to them. Nothing
harms our culture *more* than the superfluity of presumptuous loafers

and fragmentary humanitarianisms; our universities, *against* their will, are the real hothouses for this kind of instinctual atrophying of the mind. And the whole of Europe already has a notion of it—great politics deceives no one . . . Germany is being seen more and more as Europe's *flatland*.* I am still *searching* for a German with whom *I* could be serious in my way—how much more am I searching for one with whom I might be cheerful! *Twilight of the idols*: oh who would understand nowadays *what seriousness* a hermit is recovering from here!—Cheerfulness is our most incomprehensible feature . . .

4

Let us draw up a provisional balance: it is not only patently clear that German culture is in decline; there is no lack of sufficient reason* for it, either. In the last resort no one can expend more than he has—that is true of individuals; it is true of nations. If you expend yourself on power, great politics, the economy, world trade, parliamentarianism, military interests—if you give away the quantity of reason, seriousness, will, self-overcoming* that you are in *this* direction, then on the other side there is a lack. Culture and the state—let no one deceive himself here—are antagonists: 'cultural state' is just a modern idea.* The one lives off the other, the one flourishes at the expense of the other. All great periods in culture are periods of political decline: anything which is great in a cultural sense was unpolitical, even *antipolitical*.—Goethe's heart opened up at the phenomenon of Napoleon—it *closed up* at the 'Wars of Liberation'* . . . At the same moment as Germany is rising up as a great power, France is gaining a new importance as a *cultural power*. By now a great deal of new intellectual seriousness and *passion* has already moved over to Paris: the question of pessimism, for example, the question of Wagner,* practically all psychological and artistic questions are given incomparably more sensitive and thorough consideration there than in Germany—the Germans are even *incapable* of this kind of seriousness.—In the history of European culture the rise of the 'Reich' means one thing above all: a *shift in emphasis*. People everywhere already know: in the area of principal importance—and that is still culture—the Germans are no longer worth considering. People ask: have you even just one mind to show for yourself which *counts* for Europe, in the way that your Goethe, your Hegel,* your Heinrich

Heine,* your Schopenhauer counted?—The fact that there is not a
single German philosopher left never ceases to amaze.*—

5

The whole system of high-school education in Germany has lost sight
of the most important thing: the *end* as well as the *means* to the end.
That schooling, *education** is an end in itself—and *not* 'the Reich'—
that to this end *educators* are needed—and *not* grammar-school
teachers or university scholars—people have forgotten this . . . What
is needed is educators *who have educated themselves*: superior, noble
minds, proven at every moment, proven by their words and silences,
mature cultures grown *sweet**—*not* the learned louts whom grammar
school and university serve up to the youth of today as 'higher nurse-
maids'. Apart from the rarest of exceptions, educators—the *foremost*
precondition for education—*are lacking*: *hence* the decline of German
culture.—One of those exceedingly rare exceptions is my admirable
friend Jakob Burckhardt* in Basle: it is to him above all that Basle
owes its humanitarian pre-eminence.—What Germany's 'high
schools' actually achieve is a brutal kind of training aimed at losing
as little time as possible in making a multitude of young men usable,
exploitable for public service. 'Higher education' and *multitude*—the
two contradict each other from the outset. Any higher education
belongs only to the exception: you must be privileged in order to
have a right to such an exalted privilege. All great things, all beautiful
things can never be common property: *pulchrum est paucorum hominum*.*—What *determines* the decline of German culture? The fact that
'higher education' is no longer a *prerogative*—the democratism of
'education' become 'universal', *common** . . . Not forgetting that military privileges formally guarantee *over-attendance* of the high schools,
i.e. their decline. No one is free any longer in present-day Germany to
give their children a noble education: our 'high' schools are without
exception geared to the most ambiguous mediocrity, with teachers,
teaching plans, teaching objectives. And everywhere an indecent
haste prevails, as though something would be missed if the young
man of 23 were not yet 'finished', did not yet know the answer to the
'main question': *which* occupation?—A higher kind of man, if I may
be forgiven for saying so, does not like 'occupations', precisely
because he knows he has a calling* . . . He has time, he takes his

time, he does not even think of getting 'finished'—at thirty you are, in the sense of high culture, a beginner, a child.—Our overcrowded grammar schools, our overwhelmed and stupefied grammar-school teachers, are a scandal: to stand up for these conditions, as the Heidelberg professors have recently done, you might perhaps have *cause*—but there are no grounds for it.

6

In order not to be untrue to my type, which is *yea-saying* and will only have anything to do with contradiction and criticism indirectly and when forced to, I shall describe at once the three tasks for which educators are needed. You have to learn to *see*, you have to learn to *think*, you have to learn to *speak* and *write*: in all three cases the goal is a noble culture.—Learning to *see*—accustoming the eye to rest, to patience, to letting things come to it; learning to defer judgement, to encircle and encompass the individual case on all sides.* This is the *first* preparatory schooling for intellectuality: *not* to react immediately to a stimulus, but to take in hand the inhibiting, isolating instincts. Learning to *see*, as I understand it, is almost what is called in un-philosophical language 'strong will': the most important thing about it is precisely *not* to 'will', to be *able* to defer decision. Every lack of intellectuality, every vulgarity is based on the inability to resist a stimulus—you *must* react, you follow every impulse. In many cases such a necessity is already sickliness, decline, a symptom of exhaustion—almost everything which coarse, unphilosophical language calls by the name of 'vice' is merely this physiological inability *not* to react. One lesson from having learnt to see: as a *learner* you will have become generally slow, mistrustful, reluctant. You will initially greet any kind of alien, *new* thing with a hostile calm, and let it approach—you will draw your hand back from it. Opening all your doors, subserviently prostrating yourself before every little fact, stepping, *rushing* into one thing after another, ever ready to pounce, in short our famous modern 'objectivity' is bad taste, *ignoble par excellence*.—

7

Learning to *think*: in our schools people no longer have any notion of it. Even in the universities, even among the true scholars of philosophy, logic as theory, as practice, as *craft* is beginning to die out. If you read German books you find not the faintest memory of the need for a technique, a teaching plan, a will to mastery in thinking—of the fact that thinking needs to be learned just as dancing needs to be learned, *as* a kind of dancing . . . Who is there among Germans who knows from experience that slight shiver which spreads out to all the muscles from *light feet* in intellectual matters! Ungainly, boorish intellectual gestures, *clumsy* hands in grasping— these are so German that people abroad confuse them with the very essence of being German. Germans have no *fingers* for nuances . . . The fact that the Germans have even just endured their philosophers, above all that most stunted conceptual cripple ever, the *great* Kant,* is no mean indication of German grace.*—For you cannot subtract every form of *dancing* from *noble education*, the ability to dance with the feet, with concepts, with words; do I still need to say that you must also be able to dance with the *pen*—that you must learn to *write*?—But at this point I would become a complete riddle to German readers . . .

RECONNAISSANCE RAIDS* OF AN UNTIMELY MAN

I

My Impossibles.—*Seneca*: or the toreador of virtue.*—*Rousseau*:* or the return to nature *in impuris naturalibus*.*—*Schiller*: or the Morality-Trumpeter of Säckingen.*—*Dante*: or the hyena who *versifies* in graves.*—*Kant*: or cant* as intelligible character.*—*Victor Hugo*: or the pharos by the sea of nonsense.*—*Liszt*:* or the School of Velocity—after women.*—*George Sand*:* or *lactea ubertas*,* in plain words: the milk cow with 'beautiful style'.*—*Michelet*:* or enthusiasm taking its jacket off . . . *Carlyle*:* or pessimism as lunch revisited.—*John Stuart Mill*:* or offensive clarity.—*Les frères de Goncourt*: or the two Ajaxes struggling with Homer.* Music by Offenbach.*—*Zola*: or 'the joy of stinking'.*—

2

Renan.—Theology, or the ruination of reason by 'original sin' (Christianity). Witness Renan who, whenever he risks a yes or a no of a more general kind, misses the mark with embarrassing regularity. He would like, for instance, to merge *la science* and *la noblesse** into one: but *la science* belongs to democracy, that much is palpable. He wants, with no mean ambition, to represent an aristocracy of the mind: but at the same time he falls on his knees before the contrary doctrine, the *évangile des humbles*,* and not just on his knees . . . What use is all freethinking, modernity, mockery, and wrynecked adroitness, if with your innards you are still a Christian, a Catholic, and even a priest! Renan's inventiveness, just like a Jesuit's and father confessor's, lies in seduction; his spirituality does not lack the broad smirk of the cleric—like all priests he becomes dangerous only when he falls in love. He has no equal in the life-threatening way he worships . . . This mind of Renan's, an *enervating* mind, is one more disastrous stroke of fate for poor, sick, will-sick France.—

3

*Sainte-Beuve.**—Nothing manly about him; full of petty rage
against all manly spirits. Roves around, delicate, curious, bored,
sounding things out—fundamentally womanly, with a woman's
vindictiveness and a woman's sensuality. As a psychologist a
genius at *médisance;** inexhaustibly rich in ways of being so; no
one understands better how to lace praise with poison. Plebeian in
the depths of his instincts and related to Rousseau's *ressentiment:**
hence a Romantic—for beneath all *romantisme** Rousseau's instinct
for revenge is grunting and lusting away. Revolutionary, but still
kept fairly well in check by fear. Captivated by anything which
has strength (public opinion, the Academy,* the court, even Port
Royal*). Incensed by anything great in people and things, by
anything which believes in itself. Still poet and half-woman
enough to feel the power of greatness; constantly squirming, like
that famous worm,* because he feels constantly trodden on. As a
critic lacking a yardstick, insecure, spineless, with the tongue of a
cosmopolitan *libertin* for many things, but lacking the courage
even to confess to *libertinage.* As a historian lacking a philosophy,
lacking the *power* of philosophical vision—thus balking at the
task of judging in all the most important matters, holding up
'objectivity' as a mask in front of him. He behaves differently in
any circumstances where a delicate, effete taste is the highest
authority: then he can really brave himself and delight in himself—then he is a *master.*—In several respects prefigures Baudelaire.*

4

The *Imitatio Christi** is one of those books I cannot hold in my hands
without physiological resistance: it gives off an eternal-womanly*
parfum, for which you need to be a Frenchman—or a Wagnerian . . . This saint has a way of speaking about love which makes
even Parisian women curious.—I am told that that *cleverest* of Jesuits,
A. Comte, who wanted to lead his Frenchmen on a *detour* through
science to Rome,* was inspired by this book. I can well believe it: 'the
religion of the heart'* . . .

5

G. Eliot.*—They are rid of the Christian God and are now all the more convinced that they have to hold on to Christian morality: this is an *English* kind of consequential reasoning which we will not hold against the moralizing little woman *à la* Eliot. In England, after every little emancipation from theology people have to regain their respectability in a terrifying manner, as moral fanatics. That is the *penance* they do there.—The rest of us see things differently. If you abandon the Christian faith, at the same time you are pulling the *right* to Christian morality out from under your feet. This morality is *very* far from self-evident: this point needs highlighting time and again, English fat-heads notwithstanding. Christianity is a system, a synoptic and *complete* view of things. If you break off one of its principal concepts, the belief in God, then you shatter the whole thing: you have nothing necessary left between your fingers. Christianity presupposes that man does not—*cannot*—know what is good for him, and what is evil: he believes in God, and God alone knows these things. Christian morality is an imperative; its origin is transcendental; it is beyond any criticism, any right to criticize; it is true only if God is truth—it stands and falls with the belief in God.—If the English really do believe they know by themselves, 'intuitively', what is good and evil, if they therefore think they no longer need Christianity as a guarantee of morality, then this is itself merely the *consequence* of the dominance of Christian value judgements and an expression of the *strength* and *depth* of this dominance: with the result that the origin of English morality has been forgotten, and the highly qualified nature of its right to exist is no longer felt. For the English, morality is not yet a problem . . .

6

George Sand.—I was reading the opening *Lettres d'un voyageur:** false, contrived, windy, overblown, like everything that stems from Rousseau. I cannot stand this mottled wallpaper style, or the plebeian ambitions to have generous feelings. But the worst thing remains the womanly flirtatiousness with manly features, with the manners of ill-bred youths.—How cool she must have kept through all that, this insufferable *artiste*! She wound herself up like a clock—and wrote . . . Cool, like Hugo, like Balzac,* like all the Romantics once they started writing! And how smugly she must have lain there, this fertile cow of a writer, who had something German about her in the worst sense, like Rousseau himself, her master, and who at any rate only became possible with the decline in French taste!—But Renan admires her* . . .

7

Morality for Psychologists.—Do not go in for any colportage psychology! Never observe for observing's *sake*! That gives you a false perspective, a squint, something forced and exaggerating. Experience as *wanting* to experience—that does not work. You *must* not look at yourself in your experiences,* or else every look then has the 'evil eye'. A born psychologist instinctively takes care not to look for looking's sake; the same applies to the born painter. He never works 'after nature'*—he leaves it to his instinct, his *camera obscura*,* to sift through and express the 'case', 'nature', the thing 'experienced' . . . He first becomes conscious of the *general*, the conclusion, the result: that arbitrary process of abstracting from the individual case is alien to him.—What happens if you do it differently? For instance, if you go in for colportage psychology after the manner of the Parisian *romanciers*,* big and small? *It* lies in wait for reality, so to speak; *it* brings a handful of curiosities home with it every evening . . . But just look at what you end up with—a pile of inkblots, at best a mosaic, in every case something concocted, uneasy, garish. The Goncourts are the worst at this: they cannot string three sentences together without simply hurting the eye, the *psychologist's* eye.—Nature, appraised by art, is no model. It exaggerates, it distorts, it leaves gaps. Nature is *chance*. Studying 'after nature' strikes me as a bad sign: it betrays subjection, weakness, fatalism—this self-prostration before *petits faits** is unworthy of the *complete* artist. Seeing *what there is*—that goes with a different species of mind, the *anti-artistic*, factual mind. You must know *who* you are . . .

8

On the Psychology of the Artist.—For there to be art, for there to be any kind of aesthetic doing and seeing, one physiological precondi-

tion is indispensable: *intoxication*. Intoxication has to have height-
ened the sensitivity of the whole machine, or else there can be no art.
All the very different kinds of intoxication have the power to do this:
above all the intoxication of sexual arousal, the oldest and most
original form of intoxication. Likewise the intoxication which accompanies every great desire, every strong emotion; the intoxication of
celebration, of competition, of the bravura piece, of victory, of any
extreme movement; the intoxication of cruelty; the intoxication in
destruction; the intoxication from certain meteorological influences,
for example the intoxication of spring; or from the influence of
narcotics; lastly the intoxication of the will, the intoxication of a
bulging, swollen will.—The essential thing about intoxication is the
feeling of increased power and plenitude. On the strength of this
feeling we give to things, we *force* them to take from us, we violate
them—this process is called *idealization*. Let us rid ourselves of a
prejudice here: idealization does *not* consist, as is commonly believed,
in subtracting or deducting little, incidental things. The decisive
factor is rather an immense *forcing out* of the main features, so that
in the meantime the rest fade away.

9

In this state we enrich everything out of our own plenitude: whatever
we see, whatever we want, we see swollen, crammed, strong, super-
charged with energy. Man in this state transforms things until they
reflect his power—until they are reflections of his perfection. This
need to transform into perfection is—art. Even everything he is not
nevertheless becomes an aspect of his delight in himself; in art man
finds enjoyment in himself as perfection.—It would be permissible
to think up a contrasting condition, a specific anti-artistry of the
instinct—a way of being which impoverished everything, thinned it
down, made it consumptive. And indeed history is rich in such anti-
artists, those starved of life: those who of necessity still have to take
things and sap them, *emaciate* them. This is the case, for example,
with the true Christian, with Pascal,* for example: a Christian who is
at the same time an artist *is not to be found* ... Let no one be childish
and raise an objection to me in Raphael,* or some homoeopathic
nineteenth-century Christian: Raphael said yes, Raphael *did* yes,
therefore Raphael was no Christian ...

10

What is the meaning of the conceptual opposition I introduced into aesthetics, between *Apollonian* and *Dionysian*, both conceived as types of intoxication?*—Apollonian intoxication keeps the eye in particular aroused, so that it receives visionary power. The painter, the sculptor, the epic poet are visionaries *par excellence*. In the Dionysian state, on the other hand, the whole system of the emotions is aroused and intensified: so that it discharges its every means of expression at one stroke, at the same time forcing out the power to represent, reproduce, transfigure, transform, every kind of mime and play-acting. The essential thing remains the ease of the metamorphosis, the inability *not* to react (—as with certain hysterics who also enter into *any* role at the slightest sign). It is impossible for Dionysian man not to understand every suggestion; he overlooks no emotional sign, he has the instinct for understanding and sensing in the highest degree, just as he possesses the art of communication in the highest degree. He adopts every skin, every emotion: he is constantly transforming himself.—Music, as we understand it nowadays, is likewise a total arousal and discharge of the emotions, and yet it is merely the remnant of a much fuller world of emotional expression, a mere *residuum* of Dionysian histrionism.* To make music possible as a specialized art-form a number of the senses, above all the kinaesthetic sense, were made inactive (at least relatively so: for to a certain extent all rhythm still speaks to our muscles): with the result that man no longer immediately imitates and represents with his body everything he feels. Nevertheless *that* is the truly Dionysian state of normality, at any rate the original state; with music it slowly becomes more specific at the expense of the most closely related faculties.

11

The actor, the mime, the dancer, the musician, the lyric poet are fundamentally related in their instincts and are actually one, but have gradually specialized and separated off from one another—even to the point of contradiction. The lyric poet stayed united with the musician the longest; the actor with the dancer.—The *architect* represents neither a Dionysian nor an Apollonian state: here it is the great act of will, the will which removes mountains,* the intoxication of the great will, that is demanding to become art. The most powerful people have always inspired the architects; the architect has always been influenced by power. In a building, pride, victory over gravity, the will to power* should make themselves visible; architecture is a kind of power-eloquence in forms, at times persuading, even flattering, at times simply commanding. The highest feeling of power and assuredness is expressed in anything which has *great style*. Power which no longer needs to prove itself; which disdains to please; which is loath to answer; which feels no witness around it; which lives oblivious of the fact that there is opposition to it; which reposes in *itself*, fatalistically, a law among laws: *this* is what speaks of itself in great style.—

12

I was reading the life of *Thomas Carlyle*,* that unwitting, involuntary farce, that heroic-moral interpretation of dyspeptic conditions.— Carlyle, a man of strong words and attitudes, a rhetor out of *need*, constantly provoked by the longing for a strong faith *and* the feeling of being incapable of it (—in which he is a typical Romantic!). The longing for a strong faith is *no* proof of a strong faith, rather the opposite. *If you have faith*, then you can allow yourself the fine luxury of scepticism: you are secure enough, firm enough, fettered enough* for it. Carlyle anaesthetizes something in himself by the fortissimo of his admiration for people with a strong faith, and by his rage against those who are less naïve: he *needs* noise. A constant and passionate *dishonesty* with himself—that is his *proprium*,* it is what makes and keeps him interesting.—Of course in England he is admired precisely for his honesty ... Now that is English; and—considering that the English are the nation of complete cant*—even fair enough, and not merely understandable. Basically Carlyle is an English atheist seeking to be honoured for *not* being so.

13

Emerson.*—Much more enlightened, more wide-ranging, more multifarious, more refined than Carlyle, above all happier ... One of those who instinctively live on ambrosia alone, who leave behind the indigestible in things. In comparison to Carlyle, a man of taste.

—Carlyle, who liked him very much, nevertheless said of him: 'he does not give *us* enough to sink our teeth into': which may be said with good reason, but not at Emerson's expense.—Emerson has that kindly and quick-witted cheerfulness which discourages all seriousness; he is absolutely unaware of how old he already is and how young he will yet become—he could say of himself in Lope de Vega's* words: 'yo me sucedo a mi mismo.'* His mind is always finding reasons to be content and even grateful; and now and then he verges on the cheerful transcendence of that worthy gentleman who returned from a lovers' rendezvous *tamquam re bene gesta*.* '*Ut desint vires*', he said gratefully, '*tamen est laudanda voluptas*.'*—

14

Anti-Darwin.*—As far as the famous 'struggle for *life*' is concerned, it seems to me for the moment to be more asserted than proven. It occurs, but it is the exception; life as a whole is *not* a state of crisis or hunger, but rather a richness, a luxuriance, even an absurd extravagance—where there is a struggle, there is a struggle for *power*... Malthus* should not be confused with nature.—But given that there is this struggle—and indeed it does occur—it unfortunately turns out the opposite way to what the school of Darwin wants, to what one perhaps *ought* to join with them in wanting: i.e. to the detriment of the strong, the privileged, the fortunate exceptions. Species do *not* grow in perfection: time and again the weak become the masters of the strong—for they are the great number, they are also *cleverer** ... Darwin forgot intelligence (—that is English!), *the weak are more intelligent* ... You must have need of intelligence in order to gain it— you lose it if you no longer have need of it. Anyone who has strength dispenses with intelligence (—'let it go!' people think in today's Germany, 'for the *Reich* must still be ours'* ...). By 'intelligence' it is clear that I mean caution, patience, cunning, disguise, great self-control, and all that is mimicry* (which last includes a large part of so-called virtue).

15

Casuistry of Psychologists.—Here is a connoisseur of human nature: why does he actually study people? He wants to seize on little advantages over them, or even big ones—he is a *politico*! . . . Over there is another connoisseur of human nature: and you say that he wants nothing out of it for himself, that he is a great 'impersonal' type.* Look more closely! Perhaps he wants an even *worse* advantage: to feel superior to people, to be able to look down on them and no longer mistake himself for them. This 'impersonal' type is a *despiser* of human nature: and that first one is the more humane species, whatever appearances may say. He at least sets himself on a par with them, he *projects* himself into them . . .

16

The *psychological tact* of the Germans seems to me to be called into question by a whole series of instances, which my modesty prevents me from listing. In one case I shall not let slip a great opportunity to substantiate my thesis: I hold it against the Germans that they were wide of the mark with *Kant* and his 'philosophy of loopholes', as I call it—he was *not* a model of intellectual integrity.—The other thing I do not like to hear is that infamous 'and': the Germans say 'Goethe *and* Schiller'*—I am afraid they even say 'Schiller and Goethe' . . . Do people still not *know* this Schiller?—There are still worse 'and's: I have heard with my own ears, admittedly only among university professors: 'Schopenhauer *and* Hartmann'* . . .

17

The most intellectual people, assuming they are the most courageous, also experience by far the most painful tragedies: but that is precisely why they honour life; because it pits against them its greatest adversity.

18

On 'Intellectual Conscience'.—Nothing seems to me rarer nowadays than true hypocrisy. I have the strong suspicion that this plant finds the gentle air of our culture unconducive. Hypocrisy belongs to periods of strong faith: where even when people were *required* to display a different faith they clung on to the faith they had. Nowadays people are letting go of it; or, as is even more common, they are taking on a second faith in addition—in each case remaining *honest*. Without doubt a far greater number of convictions is possible nowadays than before: possible, i.e. permitted, i.e. *harmless*. This results in tolerance towards oneself.—Tolerance towards oneself allows several convictions to be held: for their part these live peaceably together—they take care, like everyone nowadays, not to compromise themselves. How does one compromise oneself nowadays? By being consistent. By going in a straight line. By not being multiply ambiguous. By being genuine ... I am very much afraid that modern man is simply too idle for some vices: with the result that they are on the point of dying out. Everything evil, which depends on a strong will—and perhaps there is no evil without strength of will—is degenerating in our mild air into virtue ... The few hypocrites I have got to know were mimicking hypocrisy: like practically every tenth person nowadays, they were actors.*—

19

Beautiful and Ugly.—Nothing is more qualified, let us say *more limited*, than our feeling for the beautiful. If you tried to think of it in isolation from the pleasure humanity takes in itself, you would immediately lose the ground beneath your feet. The 'beautiful in itself'* is merely a word, not even a concept. In beautiful things, man posits himself as the measure of perfection;* in exceptional cases he worships himself in them. A species cannot *help* saying yes to itself alone in this way. Its *most deep-seated* instinct, for self-preservation and self-expansion, radiates out even from such sublimities.* Man thinks the world itself is overwhelmed with beauty—he *forgets* he is its cause. He alone has bestowed beauty on it—oh! but a very human, all-too-human beauty ... Basically man mirrors himself in things, he thinks anything that reflects his image back to him is beautiful: the judgement 'beautiful' is *the vanity of his species*... Now the sceptic might find a slight suspicion whispering in his ear the question: is the world really beautified just because man takes it to be beautiful? He has *anthropomorphized* it: that is all. But we have no guarantee, none at all, that it is man who should be singled out to provide the model of the beautiful. Who knows how he might look in the eyes of a higher arbiter of taste? Perhaps audacious? perhaps amused at himself? perhaps a little arbitrary? ... 'Oh Dionysus, you divinity, why are

you tugging at my ears?' Ariadne once asked her philosophical par-
amour during one of those famous dialogues on Naxos.* 'I find your
ears rather humorous, Ariadne: why aren't they even longer?'*

20

Nothing is beautiful, only man is beautiful: all aesthetics rests on this
naïvety; it is its *first* truth. Let us immediately add its second: nothing
is ugly except *degenerating* man—thus the realm of aesthetic judgement is delimited.—In physiological terms everything ugly weakens
and saddens man. It reminds him of decay, danger, powerlessness; it
actually makes him lose strength. You can measure the effect of ugly
things with a dynamometer. Whenever man gets depressed, he senses
something 'ugly' is nearby. His feeling of power, his will to power, his
courage, his pride—all are diminished by ugliness and increased by
beauty . . . In both cases *we reach a conclusion*, the premises for which
accumulate in immense abundance in our instinct. Ugly things are
understood as signs and symptoms of degenerescence: anything
which serves as the slightest reminder of degenerescence produces
in us the judgement 'ugly'. Any sign of exhaustion, of heaviness, of
age, of tiredness; any kind of constraint, a cramp, a paralysis; above all
the whiff, the colour, the form of dissolution, of decomposition, even
in the ultimate rarefaction into a symbol—all produce the same
reaction, the value judgement 'ugly'. A *hatred** springs up here:
who is man hating here? But there is no doubt: the *decline of his
type*. His hatred here stems from the most deep-seated instinct of the
species; in this hatred there is shuddering horror, caution, profundity, far-sightedness—it is the most profound hatred there is. That is
why art is *profound* . . .

21

Schopenhauer.—Schopenhauer, the last German to be worth considering (—to be a *European* event like Goethe, Hegel, Heinrich Heine,
and *not just* a local, 'national' one), is to the psychologist a case of the
first order: namely as a brilliantly malicious attempt to bring to bear
in the service of a nihilistic devaluation of all life* precisely the
counter-examples, the great self-affirmations of the 'will to life', the
exuberance-forms of life. He interpreted in turn *art*, heroism,

genius, beauty, great fellow-feeling, knowledge, the will to truth, tragedy as consequences of the 'denial' of the 'will', or the need to deny it—the greatest piece of psychological counterfeiting in history, Christianity excepted. On closer inspection he is simply the heir to Christian interpretation in this: except that he also managed to *approve* of what Christianity had *rejected*—the great cultural facts of humanity—in a Christian, i.e. nihilistic sense (—namely as paths to 'redemption', as prefigurations of 'redemption', as stimulants of the need for 'redemption'...)

22

I shall take one specific case. Schopenhauer speaks of *beauty* with a melancholy passion—but why? Because he sees in it a *bridge* which takes us further on, or makes us thirst to go further on ... It is to him a momentary redemption from the 'will'—it tempts us into redemption for ever ... In particular he praises it as redeeming us from the 'focus of the will', from sexuality*—in beauty he sees the procreative drive *denied* ... Strange fellow! There is someone contradicting you, and I am afraid it is nature. *Why* is there any beauty in sound, colour, fragrance, rhythmic movement in nature? What is it that *forces out* beauty?—Fortunately there is also a philosopher contradicting him. No lesser authority than the divine Plato (—as Schopenhauer himself calls him)* maintains a different proposition: that all beauty stimulates procreation*—that this is precisely the *proprium* of its effect, from the most sensual right up to the most spiritual ...

23

Plato goes further. With an innocence which requires a Greek and not a 'Christian', he says there would be no Platonic philosophy at all were there not such beautiful youths in Athens: only on seeing them is the philosopher's soul sent into an erotic frenzy from which it will not rest until it has planted the seed of all lofty things in such a beautiful soil.* Another strange fellow!—you cannot believe your ears, if indeed you can believe Plato. At least you can sense that they philosophized *differently* in Athens, above all in public. Nothing is less Greek than the conceptual cobwebbery of a hermit, *amor intellectualis dei** after the manner of Spinoza.* Philosophy after the manner of Plato would need to be defined as more of an erotic competition, as a development and internalization of the agonal gymnastics of old and its *preconditions* ... What was it that ultimately grew out of this philosophical erotics of Plato's? A new art-form of the Greek *agon*, dialectics.*—I would point out, *contra* Schopenhauer and in Plato's favour, that all the higher culture and literature of *classical* France, too, grew up on the soil of sexual interest. You can search everywhere in it for gallantry, the senses, sexual competition, 'woman'—and you will never search in vain ...

24

L'art pour l'art.*—The struggle against purpose in art is always a struggle against the *moralizing* tendency in art, against its subordination to morality. *L'art pour l'art* means: 'the devil take morality!' But even this enmity betrays the overwhelming force of prejudice. Once you take away from art the purpose of preaching morality and improving humanity, the result is still a far cry from art as completely purposeless, aimless, senseless, in short *l'art pour l'art*—a worm biting its own tail.* 'Better no purpose at all than a moral purpose!'—thus speaks pure passion. But a psychologist asks: what does all art do? does it not praise? does it not glorify? does it not select? does it not emphasize? In all these ways it *strengthens* or *weakens* certain value judgements ... Is this just incidental? a coincidence? something from which the artist's instinct remains completely detached? Or rather: is it not a prerequisite for the artist *to be able* ...? Is his most deep-seated instinct for art, or is it not rather for the meaning of art, *life*, for a *desideratum of life*?—Art is the great stimulant to life:* how could one conceive of it as purposeless, aimless, *l'art pour l'art*?—One question remains: art also reveals much that is ugly, harsh, questionable in life—does it not thereby seem to remove the suffering from life?—And indeed there have been philosophers who have given it this meaning: 'freeing oneself from the will' was what Schopenhauer taught as the overall purpose of art, 'fostering a mood of resignation' was what he admired as the great benefit of tragedy.*—But this, as I have already indicated, is a pessimist's perspective and an 'evil eye'—we must appeal to the artists themselves. *What does the tragic artist communicate about himself?* Is it not precisely the state of *fearlessness* in the face of the fearful and questionable that he shows?—This state is itself highly desirable: anyone who knows it honours it with the highest honours. He communicates it, he *must* communicate it, so long as he is an artist, a genius of communication. Bravery and unrestrained feeling in the face of a powerful enemy, or noble hardship, or a problem which makes one shudder with horror—it is this *triumphant* state that the tragic artist selects and glorifies. Faced with tragedy, the warlike element in our souls celebrates its Saturnalia;* anyone who is used to suffering, who seeks out suffering, the *heroic* person praises his existence through tragedy—to him alone the tragedian offers a draught of this sweetest cruelty.—

25

Contenting oneself with people, keeping open house with one's heart—that is liberal, but it is merely liberal.* Those hearts which are capable of *noble* hospitality are recognizable by their many drawn curtains and closed shutters: they keep their best rooms empty. Why, though?—Because they are expecting guests with whom one *cannot* 'content oneself' ...

26

We stop appreciating ourselves enough when we communicate. Our actual experiences are not in the least talkative. They could not express themselves even if they wanted to. For they lack the words to do so. When we have words for something we have already gone beyond it. In all speech there is a grain of contempt. Language, it seems, was invented only for average, middling, communicable things.* The speaker *vulgarizes* himself as soon as he speaks. —From a morality for deaf-mutes and other philosophers.

27

'This portrait is enchantingly beautiful!'* ... The literary woman, unsatisfied, excited, barren in heart and innards, constantly listening with painful curiosity to the imperative which whispers from the depths of her constitution '*aut liberi aut libri*':* the literary woman, educated enough to understand the voice of nature, even when it speaks Latin, and on the other hand enough of a vain old hen to talk secretly to herself in French, as well: 'je me verrai, je me lirai, je m'extasierai et je dirai: Possible, que j'aie eu tant d'esprit?'*...

28

The 'impersonal' have a chance to speak.—'We find nothing easier than being wise, patient, superior. We are dripping with the oil of forbearance and fellow-feeling, we are absurdly fair, we forgive everything. For that very reason we should keep a tighter rein on ourselves; for that very reason, from time to time, we should *cultivate* a little emotion, a little vice of an emotion. We may find it difficult; and between ourselves we may laugh at how it makes us look. But what's the use! We have no other kind of self-overcoming left: this is *our* asceticism, *our* penance'... *Getting personal*—the virtue of the 'impersonal'...

29

From a Doctoral Viva.*—'What is the task of any high-school education system?'—To turn man into a machine.—'By what means?'—He must learn to be bored.—'How is this achieved?' —Through the concept of duty.*—'Who is his model in this?' — The philologist: he teaches how to *swot up*.—'Who is the perfect human being?'—The public servant.—'Which philosophy gives the highest formula for the public servant?'—Kant's: the public servant as thing in itself set in judgement over the public servant as appearance.—

30

The Right to Stupidity.—The weary, slow-breathing worker who looks around good-naturedly and lets things go their own way:* this typical figure whom you come across now, in the age of work (*and* of the 'Reich'!—), in all social classes,* is laying claim these days to *art*, of all things, including books, above all magazines—and even more to the beauties of nature, Italy ... The man of the evening, with the 'nodding wild drives' of which Faust* speaks, needs the freshness of summer, sea-bathing, glaciers, Bayreuth* . . . In such ages art has a right to *pure folly** —as a kind of vacation for the spirit, the mind, and the soul. Wagner understood this. *Pure folly* restores one's health . . .

31

*Another Problem of Diet.**—The means by which Julius Caesar* protected himself against minor ailments and headaches: immense marches, the simplest of ways of life, uninterrupted periods in the open air, constant exertions—these are by and large the definitive measures for preserving and protecting against the extreme vulnerability of that subtle machine working under the most intense pressure, called genius.—

32

The Immoralist Speaks.—Nothing offends against a philosopher's taste *more* than man, *in so far as he desires* . . . If he sees man only in action, if he sees this most courageous, cunning, tenacious of animals lost in even labyrinthine difficulties, how admirable man seems to him! He still encourages him . . . But the philosopher despises the man who desires, as well as the 'desirable' man—and in general all man's desiderata, all his *ideals*. If a philosopher could be a nihilist, then it would be because he had discovered the nothingness behind all man's ideals. Or not even the nothingness—but merely the worthlessness, absurdity, sickness, cowardliness, weariness, all the kinds of dregs in the *drained* cup of his life . . . How is it that man, who is so admirable as a reality, deserves no respect in so far as he desires? Must he atone for making such a good job of being real? Must he compensate for his actions, the exertion of mind and will involved in every action, by stretching his limbs in the realm of the imaginary and the absurd?—The history of man's desiderata has been his *partie honteuse** thus far: one should be careful not to spend too long reading it. What justifies man is his reality—it will justify him eternally. How much more is a real person worth in comparison to some mere wished-up, dreamed-up, stinking lie of a person? to some *ideal* person? . . . And only the ideal person offends against the philosopher's taste.

33

Natural Value of Egoism.—Selfishness is worth as much as the physiological value of whoever is exhibiting it: it can be worth a great deal; it can be worthless and contemptible. Every single person can be considered from the point of view of whether he represents the ascendant or descendent line of life. A decision on this point gives you a criterion for the value of his selfishness. If he represents the line ascendant then his value is indeed extraordinary—and for the sake of the totality of life, which takes a step *further* with him, extreme care may even be taken in maintaining and creating the optimum conditions for him. For the single person—the 'individual', as the people and the philosophers have understood him thus far—is an error: he is nothing by himself, no atom, no 'ring in the chain', nothing which has simply been inherited from the past—he is the whole single line of humanity up to and including himself ... If he represents a development downwards, a falling-off, a chronic degeneration, or illness (—illnesses are by and large already the consequences of a falling-off, *not* the causes of it),* then he is worth little, and in all fairness he should *detract* as little as possible from those who turned out well. He is merely a parasite on them ...

34

Christian and Anarchist.—When the anarchist, as the mouthpiece of social strata *in decline*, waxes indignant and demands 'rights', 'justice', 'equal rights', then he is just feeling the pressure of his lack of culture, which is incapable of understanding *why* he is actually suffering—*what* he is poor in, in life ... There is a powerful causal drive within him: someone must be to blame for his feeling bad ... And 'waxing indignant' itself does him good, too; all poor devils take pleasure in grumbling—it gives a little rush of power. Even a complaint, making a complaint, can give life some spice and make it endurable: there is a small dose of *revenge* in every complaint; people blame those who are different from themselves for the fact that they feel bad, possibly even for their badness—as though it were an injustice, an *illicit* privilege. 'If I'm *canaille*,* then so should you be': this is the logic on which revolutions are based.—Complaining is never any good: it stems from weakness. Whether people attribute their feeling bad to others or to *themselves*—socialists* do the former, Christians, for example, the latter—it makes no real difference. What they have in common, let us say what is *unworthy* about them, too, is that someone is supposed to be *to blame* for their suffering—in short, that the sufferer prescribes himself the honey of revenge for his suffering. The objects of this need for revenge, a need for *pleasure*, are contingent causes: the sufferer will find grounds everywhere for venting his petty revenge—if he is a Christian, to say it again, then he will find them in *himself* ... The Christian and the anarchist—both are *décadents*.—But even when the Christian condemns, slanders, denigrates the '*world*', he does so from the same instinct from which the socialist worker condemns, slanders, denigrates *society*: the 'last judgement' itself is still the sweet consolation of revenge—the revolution which the socialist worker is also awaiting, only taken somewhat further in thought ... The 'hereafter' itself—why have a hereafter if it is not a means to denigrate this life? ...

35

Critique of Décadence *Morality*.—An 'altruistic' morality, a morality which has selfishness *wither away*—remains a bad sign whatever the circumstances. This is true of the individual; it is particularly true of nations. The best thing is lacking if a lack of selfishness begins to be felt. Instinctively choosing what is harmful to *oneself*, being *tempted* by 'disinterested' motives—this is practically the formula for *décadence*. 'Not seeking one's *own* advantage'—this is simply the moral fig-leaf for a quite different state of affairs, namely a physiological one: 'I can't *find* my own advantage any more' ... Disgregation of the instincts!—Humanity is finished when it becomes altruistic.— Instead of naïvely saying '*I* am now worthless', the moral lie in the mouth of the *décadent* says: 'Everything is worthless—*life* is worthless' ... Such a judgement remains a great danger in the end, for it is infectious—right across the morbid soil of society it will soon shoot up into a rampant tropical vegetation of concepts, one moment as religion (Christianity), the next as philosophy (Schopenhauerishness). The vegetation from a poisonous tree like that, grown from putrefaction, can continue for millennia to poison *life* with its fug ...

36

Morality for Physicians.—A sick person is a parasite on society. Once one has reached a certain state it is indecent to live any longer. Vegetating on in cowardly dependence on physicians and their methods, once the meaning of life, the *right* to life has been lost, should be greeted with society's profound contempt. The physicians, for their part, ought to convey this contempt—not prescriptions, but every day a new dose of *disgust* at their patient . . . Create a new kind of responsibility, the physicians', to apply in all cases where the highest interest of life, of *ascending* life, demands that *degenerating* life be ruthlessly pushed down and aside—for example in the case of the right to procreate, the right to be born, the right to live . . . Die proudly if it is no longer possible to live proudly. Death chosen freely, death accomplished at the right time, brightly and joyfully, among children and witnesses: so that a true leave-taking is still possible, when the one who is taking his leave *is still there*; likewise a true assessment of achievements and aspirations, a *summation* of life—all this in contrast to the pitiful and ghastly comedy which Christianity has made of the hour of death. One should never forget that Christianity has abused the dying man's weakness in order to violate his conscience, that it has abused the very way he dies and turned it into value judgements about the man and his past!—Here we must defy all the cowardlinesses of prejudice and establish above all the correct, i.e. physiological appreciation of so-called *natural* death: which is ultimately just another 'unnatural' one, a suicide. One never perishes at the hand of anyone but oneself. Only it is death under the most contemptible conditions, a death which is not free,* a death at the *wrong* time, a coward's death. For love of *life*—one ought to want death to be different, free, conscious, no accident, no ambush . . . Finally a word of advice for those pessimist gentlemen and other *décadents*. We have no power to prevent our being born: but we can make up for this mistake—and sometimes it is a mistake.* If you *do away* with yourself then you are doing the most admirable thing there is: it almost earns you the right to live . . . Society—what am I saying!—*life* itself benefits more from this than from any 'life' of renunciation, anaemia, and other virtues—you have spared other people the sight of you, you have spared life one of its *objections* . . . Pessimism—*pur, vert** pessimism—*is proved solely* by the self-refutation of those pessimist gentlemen: one must take its logic a step further, and not simply deny life with 'will and representation',* as Schopenhauer did—one must *deny Schopenhauer first of all*... Pessimism, incidentally, for all its infectiousness, nevertheless does not increase the sickliness of an age or a generation as a whole: it is its expression. One falls victim to it as one falls victim to cholera: one must already be in a morbid enough state for it. Pessimism itself does not produce a single extra *décadent*; I would draw attention to the statistical result that the total number of deaths in years when cholera is raging is no different from in other years.

37

Whether We Have Become More Moral.—My concept of 'beyond good and evil', as was to be expected, has had levelled against it all the *ferocity* of moral stultification which in Germany is known to pass for morality itself: I could tell some charming tales about this. Above all I was given to consider the 'undeniable superiority' of our time in its moral judgements, the real *progress* we had made here: I was told that in comparison with *us*, one could not possibly set up a Cesare Borgia* as a 'higher man', a kind of *overman*,* as I do... A Swiss editor, the editor of the *Bund*,* went so far—not without expressing his respect for the courage it needed to be so bold—as to 'understand' the meaning of my work as an attempt to do away with all decent feelings. Much obliged!*—I shall allow myself, in reply, to raise the question as to *whether we really have become more moral*. The fact that everybody believes this is already an objection to it... We modern men—very delicate, very vulnerable, showing and being shown a hundred kinds of consideration—actually imagine that this tender humanity which we represent, this *achieved* unanimity in being merciful, ready to help, mutually trusting, is a positive advance, and that it takes us far beyond the men of the Renaissance.* But every period thinks like that, *has to* think like that. What is certain is that we ought not to put ourselves—or even think ourselves—into Renaissance conditions: our nerves would not be able to stand that reality, let alone our muscles. Yet this incapacity is no proof of progress, but merely of a different, more belated constitution, a weaker, more tender, more vulnerable one from which a morality *full of consideration* is bound to be produced. If we imagined how we

would be without our delicacy and belatedness, without our physiological ageing, then our morality of 'anthropomorphization' would
immediately lose its value—no morality has any value in itself—
and we would even disparage it. On the other hand let us have no
doubts that we moderns, with our thickly padded humaneness which
tries to avoid bumping against a single stone, would provide the
contemporaries of Cesare Borgia with a killingly funny comedy. In
fact we are unintentionally hilarious with our modern 'virtues'...
The waning of our hostile and mistrust-instilling instincts—which
is supposed to be our 'progress'—represents just one of the consequences of the general waning of *vitality*; it takes a hundred
times more effort and care to make such a qualified, belated existence succeed. People help one another; to a certain extent everyone
is an invalid, everyone a nurse. This, then, is called 'virtue'—people
who knew life differently, as fuller, more extravagant, more overflowing, would have called it something different, perhaps 'cowardice', 'wretchedness', 'old wives' morality'...Our mitigation of
morality—this is my proposition; this is, if you will, my *innova-
tion*—is a consequence of decline; by contrast, harshness and terror
in morality can be a consequence of the surplus of life: for in this case
much can be ventured, much challenged, much *squandered*, too.
What used to be the spice of life would be *poison* for us...To be
indifferent—which is also a form of strength—we are likewise too
old, too belated: our morality of fellow-feeling, everything that one
could call *l'impressionisme morale*,* which I was the first to warn
against, is one more expression of the physiological oversensitivity
proper to everything *décadent*. That movement which tried to
demonstrate its scientific status with Schopenhauer's *morality of
sympathy**—a most unfortunate attempt!*—is the true *décadence*
movement in morality, and as such it is profoundly related to Christian morality. Periods of strength, *noble* cultures, see something
contemptible in sympathy, in 'loving one's neighbour',* in a lack of
self and self-esteem.—Periods should be measured by their *positive
energies*—in which case that Renaissance period, so extravagant and
fateful, emerges as the last *great* period, and we, we moderns with our
anxious self-welfare and brotherly love, with our virtues of work,
unpretentiousness, abiding by the law, scientificity—accumulative,
economical, machine-like—emerge as a *weak* period...Our virtues
are determined, *provoked* by our weakness...'Equality', a certain

actual assimilation, which the theory of 'equal rights' merely
expresses, is of the essence of decline:* the gulf between man and
man, rank and rank; the multiplicity of types; the will to be oneself, to
stand out—everything I call *pathos of distance**—is proper to every
strong period. The tension, the span between extremes is getting
smaller and smaller these days—ultimately the extremes themselves
are becoming so blurred as to resemble each other . . . All our political
theories *and* state constitutions—the 'German Reich' by no means
excepted—are derivatives, necessary consequences, of decline; the
unconscious effect of *décadence* has mastered even the ideals of
specific sciences. My objection to the whole of English and French
sociology remains the fact that it knows by experience only the
structures of decay in society and, in all innocence, takes its own
instincts for decay as the *norm* for sociological value judgements.
Declining life, the waning of any organizing energy, i.e. any dividing,
gulf-opening, sub- and superordinating energy, is formulated by
today's sociology into an *ideal* . . . Our socialists are *décadents*, but
Mr Herbert Spencer* is also a *décadent*—he sees the triumph of
altruism as desirable! . . .

38

My Idea of Freedom.—The value of a thing sometimes depends not
on what we manage to do with it, but on what we pay for it—what it
costs us. Let me give an example. Liberal institutions stop being
liberal as soon as they have been set up: afterwards there is no one
more inveterate or thorough in damaging freedom than liberal institutions. Now we know *what* they achieve: they undermine the will to
power, they are the levelling of mountain and valley elevated to the
status of morality, they make things petty, cowardly, and hedon-
istic—with them the herd animal* triumphs every time. Liberalism:
in plain words *herd-animalization* . . . While these same institutions
are still being fought for, they produce quite different effects: then
they are actually powerful promoters of freedom. On closer inspection, it is war that produces these effects, war waged *for* liberal
institutions, which as war allows the *illiberal* instincts to persist.
And war is an education in freedom. For what is freedom! Having
the will to be responsible to oneself. Maintaining the distance which
divides us off from each other. Becoming more indifferent towards

hardship, harshness, privation, even life itself. Being prepared to sacrifice people to one's cause—oneself included. Freedom means that the manly instincts which delight in war and victory rule over other instincts, for example the instincts for 'happiness'. The *liberated* man—and the liberated *spirit* even more so—tramples over the contemptible kind of well-being that shopkeepers, Christians, cows, women, Englishmen, and other democrats dream about. The free man is a *warrior*.—How is freedom measured, in individuals as well as nations? By the resistance which must be overcome, the effort it costs to stay *on top*. The highest type of free men would need to be sought in the place where the greatest resistance is constantly being overcome: a short step away from tyranny, right on the threshold of the danger of servitude. This is psychologically true, if one understands here by 'tyrants' pitiless and terrible instincts which require the maximum of authority and discipline to deal with them—finest type Julius Caesar—and it is also politically true, if one simply takes a walk through history. The nations which were worth something, *became* worth something, never did so under liberal institutions: it was *great danger* that turned them into something worthy of respect, the kind of danger without which we would not know our instruments, our virtues, our defences and weapons, our *spirit*—which *forces* us to be strong . . . *First* principle: you must need to be strong, or else you will never become it.—Those great hothouses for strong, for the strongest kind of people there has yet been—the aristocratic communities such as Rome and Venice—understood freedom in exactly the same sense as I understand the word freedom: as something which one can have and *not* have, which one can *want*, which one can *conquer* . . .

39

Critique of Modernity.—Our institutions are no longer any good: this is universally accepted. But it is not their fault, it is *ours*. Once we have lost all the instincts from which institutions grow, we lose the institutions themselves because *we* are no longer good enough for them. Democratism has always been the form taken by organizing energy in decline: in *Human, All Too Human** I already characterized modern democracy, along with its inadequacies like 'German Reich', as the *form of the state's decay*. For there to be institutions there must be a kind of will, instinct, imperative, which is anti-liberal to the point of malice: the will to tradition, to authority, to centuries of responsibility to come, the will to *solidarity* of generational chains stretching forwards and backwards *in infinitum*. If this will is there, then something like the *imperium Romanum** is founded: or like Russia, the *only* power nowadays which has endurance, which can wait, which still has promise—Russia, the conceptual opposite of Europe's pitiful petty-statery and nervousness, which has reached a critical condition with the founding of the German Reich . . . The whole of the West has lost those instincts from which institutions grow, from which *future* grows: nothing perhaps goes against the grain of its 'modern spirit' so much. People live for today, they live very quickly—they live very irresponsibly: and this is precisely what is called 'freedom'. The thing that *makes* institutions into institutions is despised, hated, rejected: people think they are in danger of a new form of slavery whenever the word 'authority' is even just uttered. *Décadence* has penetrated the value-instinct of our politicians and political parties to such an extent that *they instinctively prefer* anything which dissolves things, which hastens the end . . . Witness *modern marriage*. Modern marriage has patently lost all its rationality: and yet this is no objection to marriage, rather to modernity. The rationality of marriage lay in the sole legal responsibility of the husband: this is what gave marriage its centre of gravity; whereas nowadays it has a limp in both legs. The rationality of marriage lay in the principle of its indissolubility: this gave it an accent which, set against the contingencies of feeling, passion, and the moment, could *make itself heard*. Likewise it lay in the responsibility of families for the choice of husband and wife. The increasing indulgence shown towards *love*-matches has practically eliminated the basis for marriage, the thing which *makes* it an institution in the first place. An institution can never ever be founded on an idiosyncrasy; marriage, as I have already said, can *not* be founded on 'love'—it is founded on the sexual drive, on the drive to own (wife and child as property), on the *drive to rule*, which is constantly organizing for itself the smallest structure of rule, the family, which *needs* children and heirs in order to keep a physiological hold, too, on the measure of power, influence, wealth it has achieved, in order to prepare for long-term tasks, for instinctual solidarity between centuries. Marriage as an institution already encompasses the affirmation of the greatest, most enduring organizational form: if society itself cannot *guarantee* itself as a whole unto the most distant generations, then there is no sense in marriage at all.—Modern marriage has *lost* its sense—consequently it is being abolished.—

40

The Labour Question.—The stupidity, the fundamental instinctual degeneration which is the cause of *all* stupidities nowadays, lies in the fact that there is a labour question. Certain things *should not be questioned*: first imperative of instinct. I completely fail to see what people want to do with the European worker, now that he has been turned into a question.* He is in much too good a position not to ask more, and more impertinently, little by little. In the last resort he has large numbers on his side. Any hope is long gone that a modest and unassuming kind of person, a Chinese type, might develop into a class here: and this would have been reasonable, it would have been nothing short of a necessity. What have people done?—Everything so as to nip even the precondition for it in the bud—the instincts which make it possible for a worker to become a class, possible *in his own eyes*, have been utterly destroyed through the most irresponsible thoughtlessness. The worker has been made fit for military service, given the right of assembly and the political franchise: no wonder the worker nowadays already feels his existence to be a plight (morally speaking, an *injustice*—). But, to repeat my question, what do people *want*? If you want to achieve an end then you have to want the means as well: if you want slaves then you are a fool to educate them into masters.—

41

'Freedom as I do *not* mean it . . .'.*—In an age like the present, being left to one's instincts is one more disastrous stroke of fate. These instincts contradict, impede, destroy one another; I have already defined the *modern* as physiological self-contradiction. Rationality in education would want at least one of these instinct systems to be put under intense pressure and *paralysed* so as to allow another to fortify itself, to become strong, to dominate. Nowadays one would have to make the individual possible by first *cutting him back*:

possible, i.e. *whole* ... The opposite is happening: the most passionate demand for independence, free development, *laisser-aller*, is
coming precisely from those for whom no rein would be *too tight*—
this is true *in politicis*;* it is true in art. But it is a symptom of
décadence: our modern concept of 'freedom' is yet more proof of
instinctual degeneration.—

42

Where Belief is Needed.—Nothing is rarer among moralists and saints
than integrity; they may say the opposite, they may even *believe* it.
For if a belief is more useful, more effective, more convincing than
conscious hypocrisy, then instinctively hypocrisy immediately turns
into *innocence*: first proposition for understanding great saints. In the
case of philosophers, too—a different kind of saint*—their whole
trade requires them to permit only certain truths: namely those for
which their trade is *publicly* sanctioned—in Kantian language, truths
of *practical* reason.* They know what they *have* to prove, in this they
are practical—they recognize one another by the fact that they agree
on 'the truths'.—'Thou shalt not lie'—in plain words: take care, my
dear philosopher, *not* to speak the truth ...

43

A Word in the Conservatives' Ear.—What we did not know before,
what we know today, could know today—a *regression*, an about-turn
of any kind or to any extent, is just not possible. At least we physiologists know this. But all the priests and moralists have believed it
is—they *wanted* to bring humanity, *crank* humanity back to an *earlier*
measure of virtue. Morality has always been a Procrustean bed.*
Even the politicians have imitated the preachers of virtue in this
respect: even today there are still parties which dream of the crab-like
retrogression of all things as their goal. But no one is free to be a crab.*
It is no use: we *have* to go forwards, i.e. *step by step further in*
décadence (—this being *my* definition of modern 'progress' ...).
You can *check* this development and, by checking it, dam up, accumulate degeneration itself, making it more vehement and *sudden*: no
more can be done.—

44

My Idea of Genius.—Great men, like periods of greatness, are explosives storing up immense energy; historically and physiologically speaking, their precondition is always that they be collected, accumulated, saved, and preserved for over a long period—that there be a long period without explosions.* Once the tension in the mass becomes too great, then the most accidental stimulus is enough to bring 'genius', 'action', a great destiny into the world. What, then, do the environment, the age, the 'spirit of the age', 'public opinion' have to do with it!—Take the case of Napoleon. Revolutionary France, and pre-Revolutionary France even more so, would have produced the opposite type to Napoleon: indeed it *did* produce it. And because Napoleon was *different*, the heir to a stronger, longer-lasting, older civilization than the one which was going to pieces and up in smoke in France, he became master there—he *was* the sole master there. Great people are necessary, the age in which they appear is incidental; if they almost always become master of it, then this is simply because they are stronger and older, and result from a longer period of accumulation. The relationship between a genius and his age is like that between strong and weak, or old and young: the age is always comparatively much younger, thinner, more immature, more insecure, more childish.—The fact that people think *very differently* about this in France today (in Germany, too: but that means nothing), the fact that the theory of *milieu*,* a real neurotics' theory, has become sacrosanct and almost scientific there, and is believed in even among physiologists, 'does not smell good'; it makes one sad to think about it.—In England, too, they understand things no differently, but no one will be saddened by that. The English have only two ways of accommodating the genius and the 'great man': either *democratically*, after the manner of Buckle,* or *religiously*, after the manner of Carlyle. The *danger* that lies in great people and periods of greatness is extraordinary; every kind of exhaustion, and sterility, follow in their footsteps. The great person is an end; the period of greatness, for example the Renaissance, is an end. The genius—in his works, in his deeds—is necessarily a squanderer: his greatness lies in his *expenditure* ... The instinct for self-preservation is, so to speak, unhinged; the overwhelming pressure of the energies streaming out from him forbids him any such care and caution. People call

this 'self-sacrifice'; they praise his 'heroism', his indifference towards
his own well-being, his devotion to an idea, a great cause, a fatherland: all of these are misunderstandings . . . He streams out, he over-
flows, he consumes himself, he does not spare himself—fatefully,
fatally, involuntarily, just as a river bursts its banks involuntarily. But
because we owe a great deal to such explosives, we have given them a
great deal in return, too, for example a kind of *higher morality* . . . For
that is how humanity expresses its gratitude: it *misunderstands* its
benefactors.—

45

The Criminal and What is Related to Him.—The criminal type is the
type of the strong person under unfavourable conditions, a strong
person made sick. He lacks a wilderness, a certain freer and more
dangerous nature and form of existence, where all that is weapon and
defence in the instinct of the strong person *exists aright*. His *virtues*
are proscribed by society; the most vital drives he has brought with
him immediately get caught up with the depressive emotions, with
suspicion, fear, dishonour. But this is practically the *recipe* for
physiological degeneration. Anyone who has to do what he can do
best, what he would most like to do, in secret, with long periods of
tension, caution, cunning, becomes anaemic; and because he only
ever reaps danger, persecution, disastrous strokes of fate from his
instincts, even his feelings turn against these instincts—he feels
fatalistic towards them. It is society, our tame, mediocre, castrated
society, that makes a natural person who comes from the mountains
or from maritime adventures necessarily degenerate into a criminal.
Or almost necessarily: for there are cases in which such a person
shows himself to be stronger than society: Napoleon the Corsican is
the most famous case. For the problem at issue here the testimony of
Dostoevsky* is significant—Dostoevsky, the only psychologist, incidentally, from whom I had anything to learn: he was one of the most
splendid strokes of luck in my life, even more than my discovery of
Stendhal.* This *profound* person, who was right ten times over in his
scant regard for the superficial Germans, had a very different experience of the Siberian convicts in whose midst he lived for a long
time—nothing but hardened criminals for whom there was no way
back to society left—to what he himself had expected: roughly, that

they were made of the best, sternest, and most precious stuff ever produced by Russian soil. Let us generalize from the case of the criminal and think of types who for some reason lack public approval, who know that people do not find them beneficial or useful—that Chandala* feeling, that people see you not as equal but as outcast, unworthy, polluting. The thoughts and actions of all such types have a subterranean hue; everything about them becomes paler than with those on whose existence daylight shines. But almost all the forms of existence which we nowadays honour once lived in this half grave-like air: the scientific character, the artist, the genius, the free spirit, the actor, the merchant, the great discoverer . . . So long as the *priest* was seen as the highest type, *every* valuable kind of person was devalued* . . . The time is coming—I promise—when he will be seen as the *lowest* type, as *our* Chandala, as the most lying, indecent kind of person . . . I would draw attention to the way in which even today, under the mildest moral regime that has ever prevailed on earth, at any rate in Europe, every aberration, every long, all-too-long *underneath*, every unusual, obscure form of existence brings us closer to that type of which the criminal is the fulfilment. All innovators of the spirit bear the wan, fatalistic mark of the Chandala on their foreheads for a while: *not* because people experience them as such, but because they themselves feel the terrible gulf separating them from all that is conventional and held in esteem. Almost every genius is familiar with 'Catilinarian existence'* as one stage in his develop-ment, a feeling of hatred, revenge, and rebellion against all that already *is* and no longer *becomes** . . . Catiline—the form in which *every* Caesar pre-exists.—

46

*Here the View is Clear.**—It may be loftiness of soul when a phil-osopher keeps quiet; it may be love when he contradicts himself; it is possible for a man of knowledge to lie out of politeness. It has been said, not without subtlety: 'il est indigne des grands cœurs de répandre le trouble, qu'ils ressentent':* except one must add that being unafraid *of what is most unworthy* may equally be greatness of soul.* A woman who loves sacrifices her honour; a man of knowledge who 'loves' sacrifices perhaps his humanity; a god who loved became* a Jew . . .

47

Beauty No Accident.—Even the beauty of a race or a family, its grace and goodness in all its gestures, is worked for: like genius, it is the end result of the accumulated labour of generations. Great sacrifices need to have been made to good taste; for its sake much needs to have been done and much left undone—seventeenth-century France* is admirable in both respects—it needs to have been applied as a principle of selection for society, location, clothing, sexual satisfaction; beauty needs to have been preferred to advantage, habit, opinion, laziness. Highest guiding principle: even with yourself you must not 'let yourself go'.—Good things are exceedingly costly: and the law always applies that he who *has* them is different from the one who *acquires* them. Everything good is inherited: anything not inherited is imperfect, just a beginning . . . In Athens in the time of Cicero, to his express surprise, the men and youths were far superior to the women in beauty: but what labour and effort in the service of beauty the male sex there had demanded of itself for centuries!—Now let there be no mistake here about the methodology: a disciplining of feelings and thoughts alone counts for almost nothing (—here lies the great misunderstanding in German education, which is a complete illusion): you have to win over the *body* first. The strict maintenance of significant and select gestures, a commitment to live only with people who do not 'let themselves go', is perfectly sufficient to make you significant and select: within two or three generations everything has already been *internalized*. It is decisive for the fate of a nation and of humanity that culture is begun in the *right* place—*not* in the 'soul' (which was the disastrous superstition of the priests and semi-priests): the right place is the body, gesture, diet, physiology—the *rest* follows on from this . . . This is why the Greeks remain the *foremost cultural event* in history—they knew, they *did* what was necessary; Christianity, which has despised the body,* has so far been the greatest of humanity's misfortunes.—

48

Progress in My Sense.—Even I speak of a 'return to nature',* although it is actually not a going back but a *coming up*—up into high, free, even fearful nature and naturalness, the kind which plays—is *entitled* to play—with great tasks...To use an *analogy*: Napoleon was a piece of 'return to nature' as I understand it (for example *in rebus tacticis*,* and even more so, as army officers know, in matters strategic).—But Rousseau—where did *he* actually want to go back to? Rousseau, that first modern man, idealist and *canaille* in one person, who needed moral 'dignity' in order to stand the sight of himself; sick with unbridled vanity and unbridled self-contempt. Even this abortion, who lodged himself on the threshold of the new age, wanted a 'return to nature'—where, to repeat my question, did Rousseau want to go back to?—I still hate Rousseau *in* the Revolution: it is the world-historic expression of that duplicity of idealist and *canaille*. The bloody farce with which this Revolution played itself out, its 'immorality', is of little concern to me: what I hate is its Rousseauesque *moral*—the so-called 'truths' of the Revolution, through which it is still having an effect and winning over everything shallow and mediocre. The doctrine of equality!*...But there is no more venomous poison in existence: for it *appears* to be preached by justice itself, when it is actually the *end* of justice...'Equality to the equal; inequality to the unequal'— *that* would be true justice speaking: and its corollary, 'never make the unequal equal'. Because that doctrine of equality was surrounded by so much horror and bloodshed, this 'modern idea' *par excellence* was given a kind of glory and fiery glow, so that the Revolution as *spectacle* seduced even the noblest of minds. Ultimately that is no reason to respect it the more.—I can see only one man who experienced it as it must be experienced, with *revulsion*—Goethe...

49

Goethe—not a German event but a European one: a magnificent attempt to overcome the eighteenth century by a return to nature, by a coming-*up* to the naturalness of the Renaissance, a kind of self-overcoming on the part of that century.—He bore its strongest instincts in himself: sentimentality, nature-idolatry, the anti-historical, the idealistic, the unreal and revolutionary (—the last being merely a form of the unreal). He made use of history, natural science, antiquity, as well as Spinoza, and of practical activity above all;* he surrounded himself with nothing but closed horizons; he did not divorce himself from life but immersed himself in it; he never lost heart, and took as much as possible upon himself, above himself, into himself. What he wanted was *totality*; he fought against the disjunction of reason, sensuality, feeling, will (—preached in the most repulsively scholastic way by *Kant*, Goethe's antipode), he disciplined himself into a whole, he *created* himself . . . In the midst of an age disposed to unreality, Goethe was a convinced realist: he said yes to all that was related to him in this respect—he had no greater experience than that *ens realissimum** called Napoleon. Goethe conceived of a strong, highly educated man, adept in all things bodily, with a tight rein on himself and a reverence for himself, who can dare to grant himself the whole range and richness of naturalness, who is strong enough for this freedom; the man of tolerance, not out of weakness, but out of strength, because he knows how to turn to his advantage what would destroy the average type; the man to whom there is no longer anything forbidden except *weakness*, whether it be called vice or virtue . . . Such a *liberated* spirit stands in the midst of the universe with a joyful and trusting fatalism, with *faith* in the fact that only what is individual is reprehensible, that everything is redeemed and affirmed in the whole—*he no longer denies* . . . But such a faith is the highest of all possible faiths: I have baptized it with the name of *Dionysus*.*—

50

One could say that in a certain sense the nineteenth century has *also* striven for all that Goethe as a person strove for: a universality in understanding and approving, a readiness to let everything come to it, a reckless realism, a reverence for everything actual.* How is it that the overall result is not Goethe but chaos, a nihilistic sighing, a being-at-one's-wit's-end, an instinctual weariness which *in praxi** constantly drives it to *reach back to the eighteenth century*? (—for example as a Romanticism of feeling, as altruism and hyper-sentimentality, as femininism in taste, as socialism in politics). Isn't the nineteenth century, especially at its close, just a strengthened, *coarsened* eighteenth century, i.e. a century of décadence? In which case Goethe would have been—not just for Germany, but for the whole of Europe—just an unavailing if beautiful incident?—But great people are misunderstood if they are looked at from the miserable perspective of public benefit. The fact that one cannot reap any benefit from them *is itself perhaps an aspect of their greatness* . . .

51

Goethe is the last German I hold in reverence: he would have felt three things which I feel—we also agree about the 'cross'* . . . I am often asked why I actually write in *German*, for nowhere am I worse read than in my fatherland.* But in the end who knows if I even *want* to be read today?—To create things on which time tests its teeth in vain; to endeavour to achieve a little immortality in form, *in substance*—I have never yet been modest enough to demand less of myself. The aphorism, the apophthegm, in which I am the first among Germans to be a master, these are the forms of 'eternity'; my ambition is to say in ten sentences what everyone else says in a book—what everyone else does *not* say in a book . . .

I have given humanity the most profound book it possesses, my *Zarathustra*: I shall shortly give it the most independent one.*—

WHAT I OWE THE ANCIENTS

1

In conclusion, a word about the world which I sought to approach, and to which I perhaps found a new approach—the ancient world. Here again my taste, which may be the opposite of a tolerant taste, is far from saying yes indiscriminately: it is very loath to say yes, and prefers to say no, likes best of all to say absolutely nothing . . . This is true for whole cultures; it is true for books—it is also true for locations and landscapes. Basically there is a very small number of ancient books that count for anything in my life; the most famous are not among them. My feeling for style, for the epigram as style, was stirred almost the moment I came into contact with Sallust.* I have not forgotten the amazement of my dear teacher Corssen* when he had to give his worst pupil in Latin the best mark of all—I had finished in one draft. Terse, austere, with the greatest possible substance as its basis, a cool malice towards the 'fine phrase', and the 'fine feeling', too—I sensed myself here. One will recognize in me, even in my Zarathustra, a very serious ambition for *Roman* style, for the '*aere perennius*'* in style.—My first contact with Horace* was no different. To this day I have never had the same artistic delight in any poet as I was given from the start by one of Horace's odes. In certain languages what is achieved here cannot even be *desired*. This mosaic of words, in which every word radiates its strength as sound, as place, as concept, to the right and to the left and over the whole, this minimum in the range and number of its signs, the maximum which this attains in the energy of the signs—all this is Roman and, if I am to be believed, *noble par excellence*. All the rest of poetry becomes, in comparison, something too popular—a mere emotional garrulousness . . .

2

To the Greeks I owe no similarly strong impressions at all; and, to say it straight out, they *cannot* be to us what the Romans are. One does not *learn* from the Greeks—their manner is too alien, and too fluid, to have an imperative, 'classical' effect. Who would ever have learnt how to write from a Greek! Who would ever have learnt *without* the Romans! . . . Now let no one cite Plato here as an objection. In relation to Plato I am a thoroughgoing sceptic and have never been able to join in the admiration for Plato the *artist* which is conventional among scholars. In the last resort I have here the most refined arbiters of taste among the ancients themselves on my side. Plato, it seems to me, mixes up all stylistic forms, which makes him a *first* stylistic *décadent*:* he has on his conscience something similar to the Cynics* who invented the *satura Menippea*.* The Platonic dialogue, that dreadfully self-satisfied and childish kind of dialectics, can only have a stimulating effect if one has never read any good Frenchmen—Fontenelle,* for example. Plato is boring.—Ultimately my distrust of Plato runs deep: I find he has strayed so far from all the fundamental instincts of the Hellenes, he is so spoilt by morality, so proto-Christian*—he already has the concept 'good' as his highest concept—that to describe the whole phenomenon of Plato I would use the harsh term 'superior swindle' or, if it sounds better, idealism, in preference to any other. We have paid dearly for the fact that this Athenian received his education from the Egyptians (—or from the Jews in Egypt?* . . .) In the great disastrous stroke of fate which is Christianity, Plato is that ambiguity and fascination called 'ideal', which made it possible for the nobler types in antiquity to misunderstand themselves and step onto the *bridge* which led to the 'cross' . . . And how much Plato there still is in the concept 'church', in the structure, system, practice of the church!—My recuperation, my preference, my *cure* for all Platonism has always been *Thucydides*.* Thucydides, and perhaps Macchiavell's *principe*,* are most closely related to me through their absolute will not to fool themselves and to see reason in *reality*—*not* in 'reason', still less in 'morality' . . . For the wretched way the Greeks gloss over things with their ideal, which the 'classically educated' youth carries with him into later life as the reward for his grammar-school dressage, there is no more thoroughgoing cure than Thucydides. He needs to be turned over line by line and his hidden thoughts read as clearly as his words: there are few poets so rich in hidden thoughts. In him *Sophistic** culture, i.e. *realist culture*, reaches its perfect expression: this invaluable movement amidst the moral and ideal swindle which is just breaking out on all sides, that of the Socratic schools.* Greek philosophy as the *décadence*

of Greek instinct; Thucydides as the great sum, the last revelation of
that strong, austere, harsh actuality which was instinctual to the older
Hellene. *Courage* in the face of reality is what ultimately distinguishes
between such types as Thucydides and Plato: Plato is a coward in the
face of reality—*therefore* he takes flight into the ideal; Thucydides has
himself under control, therefore he keeps things, too, under his
control . . .

3

Sniffing out 'beautiful souls',* 'golden means', and other perfections
in the Greeks, perhaps admiring their repose in greatness, their ideal
cast of mind, their lofty naïvety*—I was protected from this 'lofty
naïvety', ultimately a piece of *niaiserie allemande*,* by the psychologist
in me. I saw their strongest instinct, the will to power, I saw them
tremble before the unbridled force of this drive—I saw all their
institutions grow out of precautionary measures designed to make
them safe from one another and from their inner *explosivity*. The
immense inner tension then discharged itself in fearful, ruthless
enmity directed outwards: the city states tore each other apart so
that the citizens of each individual one might live at peace with
themselves. People needed to be strong: danger was in the offing—
it was lurking everywhere. The splendidly supple bodiliness, the
daring realism and immoralism proper to the Hellene were a *need*,
not a 'nature'. They came only later; they were not there from the
start.* And with festivals and arts they also wanted nothing but to
feel themselves *on top*, to *show* themselves on top: these are means of
glorifying oneself, even of making oneself feared . . . Judging
the Greeks in the German manner by their philosophers, and
perhaps using the smugness of the Socratic schools to draw conclu-
sions as to *what* is fundamentally Hellenic! . . . But the philosophers
are the *décadents* of Hellenism, the counter-movement against
the ancient, noble taste (—against the agonal instinct,* against the
polis,* against the value of breeding, against the authority of convention). The Socratic virtues were preached *because* the Greeks had lost
them: excitable, timorous, unstable, play-actors to a man, they had
more than enough reasons to let themselves be preached morality.
Not that it helped: but grand words and attitudes suit *décadents* so
well . . .

4

I was the first person who, in order to understand the more ancient Hellenic instinct, when it was still rich and even overflowing, took seriously that marvellous phenomenon which bears the name of Dionysus: it can be explained only by an *excess* of strength.* Anyone investigating the Greeks, like that most profound connoisseur of their culture alive today, Jakob Burckhardt* in Basle, knew at once that this was an achievement: Burckhardt inserted into his *Culture of the Greeks** his own section on this phenomenon. If you want the opposite, then you should look at the almost laughable instinctual poverty of German philologists when they approach the Dionysian. In particular the famous Lobeck,* who crawled into this world of secret states with the respectful self-assuredness of a worm which has dried out between books, and convinced himself this made him scientific, so much so that he was nauseatingly thoughtless and child-ish—applying all his erudition, Lobeck gave us to understand that all these curiosities really did not amount to anything. In truth, he tells us, the priests may well have informed the participants in such orgies about a few things of some value: for example, that wine excites lust, that it is possible for people to live off fruit, that plants blossom in the spring and wither in the autumn. As far as that disconcerting wealth of rites, symbols, and myths of orgiastic origin is concerned, with which the ancient world is quite literally overgrown, Lobeck takes it as an opportunity to become even a shade wittier: 'If the Greeks', he says (*Aglaophamus** i. 672), 'had nothing else to do, then they laughed, leapt, and rushed around, or, since from time to time man is also so inclined, they sat down, wept, and wailed. *Others* then came along later and looked for some kind of reason for their remarkable nature; and so, in order to explain these customs, those countless festival legends and myths were created. On the other hand it was believed that that *droll activity* which now took place on festival days also belonged necessarily to the festival ceremony, and it was held to be an indispensable part of the divine service.'—This is contemptible twaddle, and no one will take people like Lobeck seriously for a moment. We are affected quite differently when we test the concept of 'Greek' which Winckelmann* and Goethe shaped for themselves, and find it incompatible with the element from which Dionysian art grows—the orgiastic. In fact I have no doubt that Goethe would have excluded anything like this in principle from the possibilities of the Greek soul. *Hence Goethe did not understand the Greeks.* For only in the Dionysian mysteries, in the psychology of the Dionysian state, is the *basic fact* of the Hellenic instinct expressed—its 'will to life'. *What* did the Hellene guarantee for himself with these mysteries? *Eternal* life, the eternal return* of life; the future heralded and consecrated in the past; the triumphant yes to life over and above death and change; *true* life as the totality living on through procreation, through the mysteries of sexuality. That is why for the Greeks the *sexual* symbol was the venerable symbol in itself, the true profundity inherent in the whole of ancient piety. Every particular about the act of procreation, of pregnancy, of birth evoked the loftiest and solemnest of feelings. In the doctrine of the mysteries *pain* is sanctified: the 'woes of the woman in labour' sanctify pain in general—all becoming and growing, everything that vouchsafes the future, *presupposes* pain . . . For the eternal joy of creation to exist, for the will to life to affirm itself eternally, the 'torment of the woman in labour' *must* also exist eternally* . . . The word 'Dionysus' means all of this: I know of no higher symbolism than this *Greek* symbolism, the symbolism of the Dionysia.* In it the most profound instinct of life, the instinct for the future of life, for the eternity of life, is felt in a religious way—the very path to life, procreation, is felt to be the *holy* path . . . Only when Christianity came along, with its fundamental resentment* *against* life, was sexuality turned into something impure: it threw *filth* at the beginning, at the precondition for our life . . .

5

The psychology of the orgiastic as an overflowing feeling of life and strength, within which even pain still has a stimulating effect, gave me the key to the concept of *tragic* feeling, which has been misunderstood as much by Aristotle as, more especially, by our pessimists. Tragedy is so far from providing any proof of the pessimism of the Hellenes in Schopenhauer's sense that it should rather be seen as its decisive refutation and *counter-example*. Saying yes to life, even in its strangest and hardest problems; the will to life rejoicing in the *sacrifice* of its highest types to its own inexhaustibility—*this* is what I called Dionysian, *this* is what I sensed as the bridge to the psychology of the *tragic* poet. *Not* freeing oneself from terror and pity, not purging oneself of a dangerous emotion through its vehement discharge—such was Aristotle's understanding of it*—but, over and above terror and pity, *being oneself* the eternal joy of becoming—that joy which also encompasses the *joy of destruction*... And so again I am touching on the point from which I once started out—the *Birth of Tragedy* was my first revaluation of all values: so again I am taking myself back to the ground from which my willing, my *ability* grows— I, the last disciple of the philosopher Dionysus*—I, the teacher of the eternal recurrence...

THE HAMMER SPEAKS

(*Thus Spake Zarathustra*, III)*

'Why so hard!'—spake the kitchen coal once unto the diamond: 'for are we not close kin?'

Why so soft? Oh my brethren, this I ask of you: for are you not—my brethren?

Why so soft, so yielding and submitting? Why is there so much denial and disavowal in your hearts? so little destiny in your gazes?

And if you will not be destinies, and inexorable ones: how could you ever join with me in—vanquishing?

And if your hardness will not flash and cut and cleave: how could you ever join with me in—creating?

For all creators are hard. And bliss must it seem to you to press your hands upon millennia as upon wax—

—Bliss to write upon the will of millennia as upon bronze—harder than bronze,* nobler than bronze. The noblest* alone is truly hard.

This new table, oh my brethren, do I set over you: become hard!— —

EXPLANATORY NOTES

1 *Twilight of the Idols*: 'Götzen-Dämmerung'. A parody of *Götterdämmerung* (Twilight of the Gods), the title given to the last music drama in his tetralogy *Der Ring des Nibelungen* (The Ring of the Nibelung) by the German composer Richard Wagner (1813–83), Nietzsche's erstwhile mentor (he had attended the first public performance of the *Ring* in August 1876) and now chief antagonist. Nietzsche decided on this title relatively late; the two references to it in the text itself were added to the ends of paragraphs (V 3 and VIII 3).

How to Philosophize with a Hammer: cf. Introduction, pp. xv–xvi. A 'divine hammer' had already made an appearance in Nietzsche's philosophy at BGE 62, in the (sculptural) context of the 'artistic refashioning of *mankind*'.

3 *cheerfulness*: in his first book, *The Birth of Tragedy*, Nietzsche had attacked the glib notion of 'Greek cheerfulness' prevalent among classical scholars (indeed he had considered entitling the work 'Greek Cheerfulness'), arguing that the ancient Greeks had won through to their apparent ('Apollonian') serenity by overcoming the darker ('Dionysian') side of their nature.

revaluation of all values: the title Nietzsche had recently adopted for the four-volume work (initially called *The Will to Power*) which he had been planning for the last three years (cf. Introduction, p. x).

seriousness: the preference expressed here for 'cheerfulness' or 'high spirits' over 'seriousness' or 'gravity' (cf. Z III, 'Of the Spirit of Gravity')—especially the seriousness of German thinkers (cf. VIII 3)—is fundamental to Nietzsche's conception of philosophy (cf. especially *The Gay Science* and VIII 7).

every 'case' is a stroke of luck: 'jeder "Fall" ein Glücksfall', a pun which also alludes to Nietzsche's recently published text *Der Fall Wagner* (The Wagner Case), a blistering attack on the musician.

increscunt animi, virescit volnere virtus: 'spirits grow, valour flourishes by wounding'. To satisfy scholarly curiosity: the phrase was coined by the Roman epic poet A. Furius Antias (first century BC) and is also recorded in the *Noctes Atticae* (Attic Nights, XIII. xi. 4) of the Roman writer Aulus Gellius (*c*. AD 130–70). Cf. I 8 for a similar sentiment.

pipe up: 'laut werden', a pun which implies 'become known' as well as the more literal sense of 'become loud'.

This work, too: i.e. like *The Wagner Case*.

the title betrays it: the title of the book was originally to have been 'Idleness of a Psychologist' ('Müssiggang eines Psychologen'), and although this was abandoned, its trace remains both here and at I 1 (cf. Introduction, pp. xix–xx).

great declaration of war: the Greek philosopher Heraclitus, much admired by Nietzsche (cf. III 2 and note to p. 16) asserted that war was 'the father of all things'. On the same day that he wrote this Foreword, Nietzsche also concluded *The Antichrist* with a 'Law Against Christianity' declaring '*Deadly war on the vice: the vice is Christianity*'. This martial tone became increasingly strident towards the end of the year, as in a similar declaration on 'Great Politics' (December) which begins simply: 'I bring war.'

3 *first book of the Revaluation of All Values*: *The Antichrist*, which Nietzsche wrote 3–30 September 1888, before adding this Foreword to *Twilight*. By the end of November 1888 he had abandoned the planned four-volume work, and 'Revaluation of All Values' had become simply the subtitle to *The Antichrist*; subsequently it fell away altogether to be replaced by 'Curse on Christianity'.

5 *Barbs*: 'Pfeile'—literally 'arrows', but also with the connotation of 'barbed remarks'.

Psychology... to do: the whole aphorism is an extended pun on the proverb 'Müssiggang ist aller Laster Anfang', literally 'idleness is the beginning of all vices'.

Aristotle: Greek philosopher (384–322 BC). The passage Nietzsche is referring to here occurs in the *Politics*, 1253a.

compound lie: literally a 'double' lie, but Nietzsche is again punning, on 'einfach' (simple, single) and 'zwiefach' (double). The saying is attributed to the Dutch physician Hermann Boerhaave (1668–1738), and (as *simplex sigillum veri*, 'simplicity is the mark of truth') was a favourite motto of Nietzsche's early mentor, Arthur Schopenhauer (1788–1860: cf. note to p. 24).

Whatever... stronger: a maxim Nietzsche reuses in *Ecce Homo* (I 2).

6 *Remorse is indecent*: a slogan which encapsulates the argument of the Second Essay in *On the Genealogy of Morals*, on '"Guilt", "Bad Conscience", and Related Matters'.

ass: the French philosopher Jean Buridan (*c.*1295–1356) popularized the example of a tragically over-philosophical ass perishing because it could not find any reason to choose between two equally desirable bales of hay, although the ass is in any case an important figure in Nietzsche's philosophical bestiary, especially in *Thus Spake Zarathustra*, where its braying ('I-A') parodies the 'yea-saying' ('Jasagen') advocated by Zarathustra. Cf. Z III, 'Of the Spirit of Gravity', and IV, both 'The Awakening' and especially 'The Ass Festival'.

only the English do that: an allusion to the ethical doctrine of utilitarianism, classically expounded by the two English political philosophers Jeremy Bentham (1748–1832) and John Stuart Mill (1806–73), in whose words 'actions are right in proportion as they tend to promote happiness'. Nietzsche is invariably critical of the movement—cf. especially BGE 228 and 253.

From a rib of his God: a typically Nietzschean inversion of a biblical event—the (second) creation of Eve, from Adam's rib (Genesis 2: 21–2). Also one of several aphorisms in this section (the others are I 14, 21, and 27) which bear the traces of Nietzsche's reading (and excerpting from) the first volume of the *Journal des Goncourt* (Paris, 1887) by the French writers, brothers Edmond (1822–96) and Jules (1830–70) Goncourt (whom Nietzsche nevertheless dismisses as two of his 'impossibles': cf. IX 1).

zeros: 'Nullen' (mathematical 'noughts', but also 'nobodies').

Posthumous people... timely ones: the distinction between 'posthumous', or 'untimely', and 'timely' is a crucial one for Nietzsche. The phrase 'some are born posthumously' is one of his most famous formulations which occurs both in the Foreword to *The Antichrist* and in *Ecce Homo* (III 1). His self-perception as 'untimely' spans his whole philosophical career, from the *Untimely Meditations* (1873–6) to the 'Reconnaissance Raids of an Untimely Man' here (IX).

pudeurs: 'modesties'. Nietzsche elsewhere develops the theme of truth's own womanly modesty, and her attempts to veil herself, especially in the Preface to *Beyond Good and Evil*. Cf. also I 25 and the theme of revelation as exposure at II 5, 7; GS, 'Preface' 4; GS 59 ff., 339.

7 *panem et Circen...*: Nietzsche adapts the famous description by the Roman writer Juvenal (AD 58/67–*c*.127) of what keeps the Roman mob happy—'panem et circenses' (bread and circuses: *Satires*, x. 81)—and turns it into 'bread and Circe', thereby turning art into the enchantress of Homer's *Odyssey*.

The complete woman... a little sin: cf. 'Reconnaissance Raids of an Untimely Man' for equally disparaging remarks on George Sand (IX 1, 6) and on 'the literary woman' (IX 27).

tightrope walker: in the Prologue to *Thus Spake Zarathustra*, Zarathustra witnesses a tightrope walker—symbolizing humanity as 'a rope fastened between animal and overman', 'a rope over an abyss'—falling to his death. Cf. Z, 'Zarathustra's Prologue' 3, 4, and 6.

'Wicked people have no songs': a slightly modified quotation from the poem 'Die Gesänge' (The Songs) by the German writer Johann Gottfried Seume (1763–1810).

Russians: if one remembers that for Nietzsche 'wicked' ('böse') is a compliment, what seems at first sight to be a cheap gibe against the Russians becomes an indirect expression of admiration. His expectation that they would play a major role in world politics in the twentieth century is reflected in IX 39.

'German spirit': ' "Deutscher Geist" '. 'Geist' is a notoriously untranslatable word, the meaning of which hovers between the primary senses 'spirit', 'mind', and 'intellect'. Nietzsche gives his inimitable 'definition' at IX 14: 'By "intelligence" [Geist] it is clear that I mean caution, patience, cunning, disguise, great self-control, and all that is mimicry (which last includes a large part of so-called virtue).' He returns to the question of 'der deutsche Geist' in 'What the Germans Lack' (especially VIII 1–3).

eighteen years: i.e. since the founding of the new German Reich in 1871. In the first of the *Untimely Meditations*, *David Strauss the Confessor and the Writer* (1873), Nietzsche is already warning against *'the defeat, indeed the extirpation of the German spirit in favour of the "German Empire"'* (UM I 1). He will again criticize the Reich more explicitly in 'What the Germans Lack' (*passim*; cf. also IX 14, 30, 37, 39).

8 *How many remorsels... question*: the whole aphorism is a pun on the German for 'remorse' or 'pangs of conscience', 'Gewissensbisse' (literally,

'conscience-bites'). Cf. GM II 15, on *morsus conscientiae*, the Latin term from which the German and English derive.

8 *A worm . . . trodden on*: Nietzsche exploits the fact that worms behave differently in German proverbs than in English ones—when trodden on, they do not 'turn' to resist, but 'squirm' to offer the least resistance on the path.

9 *God as singing songs*: refers to the popular patriotic poem by the German writer Ernst Moritz Arndt (1769–1860), 'Des Deutschen Vaterland' (The German's Fatherland), which contains the lines: 'So weit die deutsche Zunge klingt | Und Gott im Himmel Lieder singt'—i.e. 'As far as the German tongue sounds | And sings songs to God in heaven', although the grammar allows Nietzsche's humorous misreading: 'And God in heaven sings songs'. Nietzsche's friend Heinrich Köselitz (Peter Gast) missed the joke when he was sent the manuscript of *Twilight*, prompting a withering response from its author (KGB III/5, 443 f.).

On ne peut . . . assis: 'One can think and write only when sitting down'. Since the German for the ability to sit still is 'Sitzfleisch haben' (to have sitting-flesh), Nietzsche is here condemning a 'sin of the flesh'.

G. Flaubert: Gustave Flaubert, French writer (1821–80). Nietzsche found the saying reported by Guy de Maupassant (1850–93) in his Foreword to *Lettres de Gustave Flaubert à George Sand* (Paris, 1884), p. iii.

nihilist: the jocular context belies the importance of this term in Nietzsche's philosophy. Many of his notes from the 1880s are devoted to 'European Nihilism', which was to have formed one of the books of *The Will to Power* (cf. e.g. WP 2: 'What does nihilism mean? *That the highest values devalue themselves*'). The characterization of Flaubert as a 'nihilist' is borrowed from the *Essais de psychologie contemporaine* (*Essays in Contemporary Psychology*, 1883, III) by the French novelist and cultural critic Paul Bourget (1852–1935).

we immoralists: a self-description which recurs in *Twilight* (cf. V 3, 6; VI 7; IX 32) and throughout Nietzsche's late works, especially *Ecce Homo* (cf. EH III 'UM' 2; EH III 'HA' 6; EH IV 2, 4, 6). 'The Immoralist' was to have been the title of one of the books of the 'Revaluation of All Values', although in the end it was left to the French writer André Gide (1869–1951) to claim it for his story *L'Immoraliste* (1902).

anarchists: cf. IX 34, where Nietzsche attacks Christians and anarchists together ('the anarchist . . . the mouthpiece of social strata *in decline*').

10 *the apes of their ideal*: a punning allusion to Darwin's theory of evolution (cf. IX 14).

Formula . . . a goal: the 'formula' reappears as the 'Formula of our happiness' at AC 1; the 'straight line' is recommended again at IX 18.

11 *Socrates*: Greek philosopher (*c.*470–399 BC), generally accepted as the founding father of the Western intellectual tradition and hence a prime target for Nietzsche, whose simultaneous admiration for and severe criticism of Socrates as the 'theoretical man' *par excellence* is one of his constant themes, dating back to *The Birth of Tragedy* (cf. BT 12–20).

'Life . . . a cock': Plato (Socrates' most illustrious pupil, 428–347 BC) reports Socrates' dying words as being simply: 'Crito, we owe a cock to Asclepius; pray do not forget to pay the debt' (*Phaedo*, 118a), although giving Asclepius a cock usually implied recovery from an illness. In his edition of the *Phaedo*, the German classical philologist Ulrich von Wilamowitz-Moellendorff (1848–1931)—author of two venomous polemics against Nietzsche's *The Birth of Tragedy*—specifically rejects the interpretation Nietzsche prefers, arguing that Socrates is referring to a thank-offering he had earlier promised Asclepius in return for curing the illness of one of the members of his family: 'Life is not an illness, and Asclepius does not heal any sickness of the soul' (*Platon*, ii. 57 f.). Cf. GS 340.

pessimists: Nietzsche's usual shorthand for Schopenhauerians (cf. IX 36).

consensus sapientium: 'consensus of the wise'.

wisest of every age: the first of numerous quotations from and allusions to the works of Nietzsche's enduring hero, the German writer Johann Wolfgang von Goethe (1749–1832). The source here is Goethe's 'Kophtisches Lied' (Cophtic Song), l. 3: 'All the wisest of every age.' Nietzsche quotes ll. 3–7 of the same poem at HA I 110.

décadents: Nietzsche's critique of contemporary European 'decadence' is an important feature of his later works, especially in his attacks on Wagner, who serves as his model of the 'decadent' artist (cf. WC, NcW). 'Nothing has preoccupied me more profoundly than the problem of *décadence*', he writes in the Preface to *The Wagner Case*: since he adopted the term from Bourget he almost invariably uses the French word, although he also uses many similar terms such as 'Entartung' (degeneration), the Gallicism 'Degenerescenz' (degenerescence), 'Verfall' (falling-off), and 'Niedergang' (decline), all of which reinforce his general topology of 'ascending' versus 'descending' cultures.

Birth of Tragedy: Nietzsche's attitude in *The Birth of Tragedy* towards 'the divine Plato' (BT 12) is actually a good deal more conciliatory than he implies here. Cf. IX 22, where he uses 'divine Plato' again, this time making sure he ironizes it by attributing the epithet to Schopenhauer.

12 *the value of life cannot be assessed*: allusion to the book *Der Wert des Lebens* (The Value of Life, 1865) by the German philosopher Karl Eugen Dühring (1833–1921). Cf. V 5.

Socrates was rabble: Nietzsche's vocabulary for insulting 'degenerate' types is particularly rich and multilingual: not only 'Pöbel', as here, but *'canaille'* (riff-raff: IX 34, 48), 'Tschandala' (Chandala: VII 3–4; IX 45), and 'plebejisch' (plebeian: IX 3). Cf. also Z II, 'Of the Rabble' (Gesindel) and GM I 9: 'the people [Volk] have won—or the "slaves" [Sklaven] or the "plebeians" [Pöbel] or the "herd" [Herde] or whatever you want to call them.'

how ugly he was: Socrates' ugliness was indeed famed: cf. Alcibiades' speech in Plato's *Symposium* (215b).

monstrum in fronte, monstrum in animo: 'a monster in the face, a monster in the soul'.

12 *that famous... 'You know me, sir!'*: the incident is recorded by the Roman orator and statesman Marcus Tullius Cicero (106–43 BC) in his *Tusculanae Disputationes* (Tusculan Disputations, 45 BC), iv. 80.

'Socrates' Demon': in Plato's account of his trial, Socrates describes the experience as follows: 'I am subject to a divine or supernatural experience . . . It began in my early childhood—a sort of voice which comes to me; and when it comes it always dissuades me from what I am proposing to do, and never urges me on' (*Apology*, 31c–d).

idiosyncrasy: the primary sense here is medico–physiological ('physical constitution peculiar to a person').

13 *noble taste*: one whole section of *Beyond Good and Evil* is entitled 'What is Noble?', and Nietzsche returns to the question of nobility repeatedly here, especially in VIII (1, 5, 6). 'Taste' is one of his most highly prized senses: the section 'Why I Am So Wise' in *Ecce Homo* is largely devoted to it.

the rabble comes out on top: a similar inversion of perspectives, 'the slave revolt in morals', is the principal theme of the First Essay in *On the Genealogy of Morals* (cf. especially GM I 10, quoted below).

revealing: Nietzsche explains this point at greater length in the Preface to *The Gay Science*, 4: 'Today it seems to us a matter of propriety that people should not want to see everything naked, to be present at everything, to understand and "know" everything.' Cf. also I 5.

Reynard the Fox: 'Reineke Fuchs'. The eponymous hero of Goethe's epic poem (1794), where the fabled character twice escapes death through his cunning 'dialectical' speeches.

resentment: 'Ressentiment', a central concept in *On the Genealogy of Morals*: 'The slave revolt in morals begins when *resentment* itself becomes creative and ordains values: the resentment of creatures to whom the real reaction, that of the deed, is denied and who find compensation in an imaginary revenge' (GM I 10). The term has usually been translated as '*ressentiment*', indicating its French origins, although Nietzsche spells it with a capital letter here and at X 4, indicating that it has the same status as, for example, 'Degenerescenz' (cf. note to p. 11). At IX 3, by contrast, he does use the French word—in a French context ('Rousseau's *ressentiment*'). Cf. also the French quotation at IX 46, where 'ressentent' has its more neutral French sense of 'feel'.

14 *agon*: 'contest'. Another central concept, the importance of which goes back to one of Nietzsche's earliest (unpublished) writings, 'Homer's Contest' (1872). The necessity of opposition to the dynamic of 'self-overcoming' (cf. note to p. 39) is repeatedly stressed here: cf. I 8; V 3 ('One is *fruitful* only at the price of being rich in opposites'); IX 23; X 3 ('agonal instinct').

drive: 'Trieb', a word which Nietzsche uses relatively interchangeably with 'Instinkt' (instinct) to denote unconscious impulses, although the latter term is generally preferred.

no one was master of himself any more: an accusation Nietzsche levels at contemporary (especially German) culture, too, from the *Untimely Meditations* on.

Cf. VIII, *passim* and IX 41: 'These instincts contradict, impede, destroy one another; I have already defined the *modern* as physiological self-contradiction.' Self-mastery is Nietzsche's most highly prized virtue, as attested to by his lavish praise for Goethe on this account at IX 49 ('he disciplined himself into a whole, he *created* himself').

de rigueur: here, 'inescapable'.

15 *unconscious*: although in our post-Freudian age the term is commonplace, it was a relatively new coinage (as a noun) in Nietzsche's time, popularized by the German philosopher Eduard von Hartmann (1842–1906: cf. note to p. 51) and his book *Die Philosophie des Unbewussten* (The Philosophy of the Unconscious, 1869).

morality of improvement: Nietzsche elaborates on this concept in 'The "Improvers" of Humanity' (VII).

cleverest: 'Klügste'. Despite the negative connotations of the term as it is used here and elsewhere (II 10; IV 1; V 3; VIII 2; IX 4, 14), it also has more positive connotations (for Nietzsche) of 'cunning' or 'malice' (cf. 'Foreword', where 'ruse' is 'Klugheit' in the German; I 31; and especially the section of *Ecce Homo* entitled 'Why I Am So Clever').

Socrates wanted to die: the evidence of the accounts by both Plato (*Apology*, 34c–35b; *Crito*) and one of Socrates' other admirers, Xenophon (*c.*430–354 BC: *Memorabilia*, IV. viii. 6) supports this. It was also the interpretation of Nietzsche's Basle colleague Jacob Burckhardt (cf. note to p. 40) in his lectures on Greek cultural history (cf. note to p. 79).

16 *becoming*: the contrast between 'being' and 'becoming' (cf. IX 45) is one of the oldest philosophical binary oppositions. Nietzsche consistently attacks the predominance of the former term in Western metaphysics, advocating instead the 'innocence of becoming' (cf. VI 7–8).

sub specie aeterni: 'from the perspective of eternity'. A variation on the phrase ('sub specie aeternitatis') used by the Dutch philosopher Benedictus (Baruch) de Spinoza (1632–77: cf. IX 23) for a 'God's-eye view' (see e.g. his principal work, the *Ethics* (1677), V, Prop. 36).

handling . . . hands: the vocabulary of 'handling' and 'hands' here is part of Nietzsche's play on the hidden metaphorical connotations of the German term for 'concept', 'Begriff'. With his image of 'conceptual mummies' ('Begriffs-Mumien') he is turning the 'grasping' ('begreifen') of concepts ('Begriffe') into something physical ('greifen'), and hence implicitly giving the lie to the philosophers' belief that they can do away with the body and the senses. Cf. also III 5 ('handling'); IV 2; VIII 6, 7 ('logic as . . . *craft*' (*Handwerk*)); IX 5.

being: Nietzsche uses two words for 'being', 'das Seiende' and 'das Sein'. In accordance with translations of the German philosopher Martin Heidegger (1889–1976), who sets great store by the distinction (which Nietzsche generally blurs), 'das Seiende' is translated as 'being' and 'das Sein' as 'Being'.

the real world: by contrast with the 'apparent world' (cf. III 2 and 6, and especially IV).

90 EXPLANATORY NOTES

16 *Heraclitus*: Heraclitus of Ephesus (*c*.550–480 BC), Greek philosopher who held that 'all things are in flux'.

17 *Eleatics*: school of philosophers founded *c*.540 BC by Xenophanes of Colophon (570–475/470 BC), comprising most notably Parmenides of Elea (*c*. 540–480 BC) and his followers Zeno of Elea (*c*.490–430 BC) and Melissus of Samos (fifth century BC). They held that not only must being be opposed to becoming, but in the choice between the two as fundamental category of existence, being is the only logically possible option.

mistaking the last for the first: en passant, another attack on Christianity ('But many that are first shall be last; and the last shall be first': Matthew 19: 30). Nietzsche returns to a critique of causality in 'The Four Great Errors' (VI).

causa sui: 'the cause of itself/himself'.

18 *ens realissimum*: 'the most real being'. Term applied initially by scholastic philosophers to God.

brain-feverish fantasies spun out by the sick: 'Gehirnleiden kranker Spinne-weber', literally 'brain-aches of sick cobweb-spinners'. A complex pun: 'Hirn-gespinst' means 'fantasy'; 'spinnen' is not only 'to spin', but also 'to spin out'/ 'invent' *and* 'to be crazy'/'to talk rubbish'.

'I': it should be noted in this context that Sigmund Freud (1856–1939) also uses the term 'das Ich' ('the I') for what has generally been translated into English as 'the ego'. Both Nietzsche's critique here of the 'I' as construct and the notion of 'projection' below (VI 3; IX 15) would subsequently be developed by Freud.

the categories of reason: the doctrine of the ten 'categories' or 'classes' of being was first formulated by Aristotle; Kant (cf. note to p. 19) developed a twelve-part logical classification of categories of the understanding in his *Kritik der reinen Vernunft* (Critique of Pure Reason, 1781).

19 *in India as in Greece*: an allusion to the Buddhist doctrine of reincarnation (metempsychosis) and the Platonic doctrine of the migration of the soul after death to the higher sphere of the Ideas (cf. *Phaedo*).

Democritus: Democritus of Abdera (460–*c*.370 BC), Greek philosopher, prin-cipal exponent of the 'atomistic' theory (cf. VI 3; IX 33), whereby all matter consists of (unchanging, indestructible) atoms, and change is explained by their mere rearrangement.

deceitful old woman: Nietzsche is here exploiting the fact that the grammatical gender of the word for 'reason' in German ('die Vernunft') is feminine.

Concocting stories: 'fabeln', which sets up the 'Fabel' ('fable') in the next section.

Kant: Immanuel Kant (1724–1804), German philosopher, and one of Nietzsche's perennial antagonists. The allusion here is to Kant's distinction (in the *Critique of Pure Reason*) between the ('phenomenal') world of ap-pearances, which is all we can know through sense perception, and the ('noumenal') world of the 'thing in itself' ('Ding an sich': cf. note to p. 28).

The tragic artist...Dionysian: unlike the earlier reference to the 'tragic' ass (I 11), Nietzsche is using 'tragic' here in the 'strong' sense he developed in *The Birth of Tragedy*, where ancient Greek tragedy is interpreted as representing a 'pessimism of strength', with the dark, 'Dionysian' elements of nature being controlled by the 'Apollonian' veneer of 'beautiful appearance'. In Nietzsche's later philosophy the 'Dionysian' element of (intoxicated) affirmation comes increasingly to predominate in his thinking and self-perception: at IX 10 the Apollonian and Dionysian are no longer in tension but allied (the former being effectively subsumed by the latter, since both are now 'conceived as types of intoxication'), for Nietzsche now conceives the crucial opposition to be that between the Dionysian and the life-denying force of Christianity, as the final words of *Ecce Homo* make clear: 'Have I been understood?—*Dionysus against the Crucified*...' (EH IV 9). Cf. also IX 49; X 4–5.

20 *History*: 'Geschichte', which means both 'history' and 'story'/'tale'.

more incomprehensible: 'unfasslicher', literally 'more ungraspable'. Again, the extended metaphor turns 'comprehending' as 'grasping' into something more concrete (cf. note to p. 16).

it becomes a woman: as with 'reason', the 'deceitful old woman' at III 5, Nietzsche is again exploiting the fact that the grammatical gender of the word for 'idea' in German ('die Idee') is feminine.

Königsbergian: i.e. Kantian, since Kant lived all his life in Königsberg (then in East Prussia, now Kaliningrad in Russia). This reference makes it clear that the 'imperative' mentioned in the previous paragraph is the Kantian 'categorical imperative', his basis of all moral action as developed in the *Kritik der praktischen Vernunft* (Critique of Practical Reason, 1788) and first formulated in the *Grundlegung zur Metaphysik der Sitten* (Groundwork of the Metaphysics of Morals, 1785): 'Act only on that maxim which you can at the same time will to become a universal law.'

positivism: system of the French philosopher Auguste Comte (1789–1857: cf. IX 4), which recognized only empirical facts and scientifically observable phenomena, and rejected metaphysics and theology.

bon sens: 'good sense'.

free spirits: those who have liberated themselves from the shackles of previous philosophical prejudices. An important term in Nietzsche's philosophy: *Human, All Too Human* is subtitled 'A Book for Free Spirits', and 'The Free Spirit' is also the title of the second section in *Beyond Good and Evil*.

INCIPIT ZARATHUSTRA: 'Zarathustra begins', i.e. the new era inaugurated by Nietzsche's great philosophical mouthpiece. *Thus Spake Zarathustra* itself begins with a passage originally published at the end of the first edition of *The Gay Science* (342) as '*Incipit tragoedia*' (*The tragedy begins*), and concludes with Zarathustra exclaiming: 'This is *my* morning, *my* day begins: *rise up now, rise up, great noon!*' (Z IV, 'The Sign').

21 *Anti-Nature*: 'Widernatur'. 'Widernatürlichkeit' is a standard German word for 'perversity', but Nietzsche is giving the term a different stress here through his neologism.

'il faut tuer les passions': 'one must kill the passions'.

'if thine eye offend thee, pluck it out': Matthew 18: 9; Mark 9: 47 (cf. AC 45). The relevant passage in the Sermon on the Mount (Matthew 5: 29) actually reads 'if thy right eye offend thee, pluck it out'.

soil: the metaphor of Christianity as a (noxious) plant recurs at VII 4; IX 35. Cf. also AC 24, 27.

the 'poor in spirit': another quotation from the Sermon on the Mount. 'Blessed are the poor in spirit, for theirs is the kingdom of heaven' (Matthew 5: 3).

22 *La Trappe*: the Cistercian monastery in Normandy which gave its name to the Trappist order, founded there in 1664 and noted for its austere rules.

the inability not to react to a stimulus: Nietzsche develops this point later, especially at VIII 6 and also at IX 10, its affirmative, 'Dionysian' modulation.

ascetics: for Nietzsche's most sustained analysis of asceticism, cf. the Third Essay in *On the Genealogy of Morals*, 'What is the Meaning of Ascetic Ideals?'

great politics: although Nietzsche develops an apocalyptic version of this term (cf. VI 2 ('My *higher* politics'); EH IV 1: 'Only after me will there be *great politics* on earth'), here (and also at VIII 3–4) he is using it more in the sense of 'macro-politics', '*realpolitik*'.

23 *'freedom of the will'*: Nietzsche's critique of the 'will' has already begun at III 5; the reason for his sceptical inverted commas here becomes clearer in the next section: cf. VI 1, 7 ('Error of Free Will'), 8.

'God looks at the heart': cf. Luke 16: 15: 'God knoweth your hearts.'

in whom God is well pleased: cf. Matthew 12: 18: 'my beloved, in whom my soul is well pleased'.

24 *Schopenhauer... 'denial of the will to life'*: the first actual mention of the philosopher, whom Nietzsche will continue to criticize (VI 6; IX 21–2, 35–7; X 5) but also to praise (VIII 4; IX 21) throughout the rest of the book. Schopenhauer advocates the 'self-suppression of the will' in his *magnum opus*, *Die Welt als Wille und Vorstellung* (The World as Will and Representation, 1819/44), i .70, where he also argues that Christ should be interpreted as 'the symbol or personification of the denial of the will to live'.

he paints... 'ecce homo!': a complex biblical allusion, firstly to the German expression 'den Teufel an die Wand malen' ('to paint the Devil on the wall'), meaning 'to think the worst' (itself derived from the writing on the wall at Belshazzar's Feast in Daniel 5: 25), and secondly to Pilate's words ('behold the man!') as he presents Christ to the mob (John 19: 5). 'Ecce homo' would serve Nietzsche as the title for one of his later books, but he had already used it as the title for the penultimate poem in the collection 'Joke, Cunning, and Revenge', which forms the 'Prelude in German Rhymes' to *The Gay Science*.

in their image: biblical allusion to God's creation of man 'in his own image' (Genesis 1: 27). Cf. VI 3; IX 19.

25 *in view ... intentions*: 'aus Hinsichten, Rücksichten, Absichten des Lebens', a typical Nietzschean play on prefixes.

we seek our honour in being affirmative: here Nietzsche is identifying himself with the characterization of the Dionysian tragic artist at III 6. Cf. VIII 6 and also X 1, where the statement is somewhat qualified.

economy: this explicit reference to an economic model is reinforced in later sections by a vocabulary of 'expense' and 'squandering' (cf. VIII 1, 4; IX 14, 37, 44), and ultimately leads to the will-to-power model (cf. note to p. 49).

26 *Cornaro*: Lodovico (Luigi) Cornaro (1467–1566), Venetian writer. His best-selling *Discorsi della vita sobria* (Discourses on a Life of Temperance, 1558) was translated into German as *Die Kunst, ein hohes und gesundes Alter zu erreichen* (The Art of Reaching a Great and Healthy Age).

a carp: i.e. toothless.

Crede experto: 'Believe the expert!', a quotation from the epic poem on the Second Punic War (*Punica*, vii. 395) by the Roman poet Silius Italicus (AD 25/26–101). Nietzsche returns to the question of diet at IX 31 and especially in *Ecce Homo* (EH II 1).

27 *light feet*: a favourite metaphor of Nietzsche's (cf. WC 1: '"What is good is light; whatever is divine moves on tender feet": first principle of my aesthetics'), which he develops at VIII 7: 'thinking needs to be learned just as dancing needs to be learned, *as* a kind of dancing'.

28 *a spirit world*: 'eine Geister-Welt' (pun intended). Schopenhauer writes of 'the world of concepts' as 'a spirit world visible to [man's mind] alone' (*The World as Will and Representation*, ii. 16).

'thing in itself': 'Ding an sich'. Term in Kant's *Critique of Pure Reason* for the unknowable causes of our sensations, as distinct from their appearances.

horrendum pudendum: 'terrible shameful part'.

dreams as my starting point: Nietzsche is developing here the argument of a much earlier passage in *Human, All Too Human* (I 13), 'Logic of the Dream'.

after the event: 'nachträglich', a term which has come to assume a key importance in the theories of unconscious temporality proposed by Freud (cf. the 'Wolf Man' case history, *From the History of an Infantile Neurosis*, 1918) and post-Freudian psychoanalysis (cf. especially the work of Jean Laplanche).

29 *nervus sympathicus*: 'sympathetic nervous system'.

30 *World as Will and Representation*: Nietzsche gives a page reference to his German edition; the passage occurs at ii. 46 ('On the Vanity and Suffering of Life').

Pascal: Blaise Pascal (1623–62), French mathematician and philosopher who, in the wake of an intense mystical experience in 1654, became one of the greatest apologists for the Christian religion. Not surprisingly a frequent target of Nietzsche's (cf. IX 9), although in *Ecce Homo* Nietzsche waxes positively maudlin about his old sparring partner: 'I do not read Pascal but *love* him, as the most instructive of all sacrifices to Christianity' (EH II 3).

31 *the Christian virtues*: cf. 1 Corinthians 13: 13: 'And now abideth faith, hope, charity, these three; but the greatest of these is charity.'

Becoming . . . innocence: restoring this 'innocence' (Unschuld) to becoming (das Werden) is the ultimate goal of Nietzsche's 'immoralism'. 'The Innocence of Becoming' (*Die Unschuld des Werdens*, 1931) was the title given to a two-volume edition of further selections from Nietzsche's notes not included in *The Will to Power*.

the priests . . . guilty: 'the origin and the purpose of punishment' form the main subject of the Second Essay in *On the Genealogy of Morals*: 'the long history of the origin of *responsibility*' (GM II 2).

in psychologicis: 'in psychological matters'.

32 *'intelligible freedom'*: in Kant's *Critique of Pure Reason* every agent has an 'empirical' character, by which it is subject to the natural laws of causality, and an 'intelligible' character, independent of experience (cf. note to p. 43), which grounds the freedom of the subject and is the basis of moral action.

Plato: cf. *Timaeus*, 68e: 'We must therefore distinguish two types of cause, the necessary and the divine.'

causa prima: 'first cause', i.e. (especially in scholastic philosophy) God as prime mover.

33 *beyond good and evil*: allusion to Nietzsche's book of the same title.

an insight . . . formulate: in *On the Genealogy of Morals*. Cf. especially GM II 12 and III 12.

semiotics: here primarily in the medical sense of 'symptomatology', the study of the signs of disease.

34 *'blond beast'*: 'leonine' man, who first appears in *On the Genealogy of Morals* (I 11).

Law of Manu: foremost of the Hindu Dharmashastras (treatises on law), reputedly authored by Manu himself, son of the god Brahma and father of the human race. Nietzsche came across quotations from the text (in French translation) in the spring of 1888, on reading Louis Jacolliot, *Les Législateurs religieux: Manou—Moïse—Mahomet* (The Religious Legislators: Manu—Moses—Muhammad, Paris, 1876), and makes further reference to it in *The Antichrist* (13, 55–7).

Chandala: 'untouchable', the lowest caste in the Hindu social hierarchy.

35 *Book of Enoch*: 1 (Ethiopic) Enoch, one of the books of the Jewish Pseudepigrapha. Nietzsche borrows the observation from *Vie de Jésus* (Life of Jesus, Paris, 1863, p. 181) by the French writer Ernest Renan (1823–92: cf. IX 2).

the gospel preached to the poor and the lowly: allusion to Renan's description of Christianity as 'l'évangile des humbles' ('the gospel of the humble'). Cf. IX 2; WC, 'Epilogue'; AC 43; EH III 'WC' 1.

the total revolt . . . against 'pedigree': cf. GM I 10 again ('the slave revolt in morals') and especially *The Antichrist* (21–4 and *passim*), where the assertions in this dense paragraph are developed at much greater length.

36 *pia fraus*: 'pious deceit', quoted from the Roman poet Ovid (Publius Ovidius Naso, 43 BC–AD 18), *Metamorphoses* (ix. 711), where it has the sense of 'white lie': Nietzsche turns it round to mean 'deceit of the pious'. Cf. BGE 105.

Confucius: K'ung fu-tzu, Chinese philosopher (551–479 BC), whose highly conservative moral doctrine, recorded by his disciples in the *Lun yü* (Analects), advocates conformity to a naturalized and immutable social hierarchy.

37 *The new Germany*: i.e. the (Second) German Reich, founded 18 January 1871 with the proclamation of King Wilhelm I of Prussia as German Emperor.

the nation of thinkers: allusion to the phrase 'the land of poets and thinkers', which had become attached to Germany in the first half of the nineteenth century (hence the enquiry about philosophers and poets just afterwards).

'Deutschland, Deutschland über Alles': 'Germany, Germany above all', first line of the 'Lied der Deutschen' (Song of the Germans, 1841) by the German poet Heinrich Hoffmann von Fallersleben (1798–1874), adopted as the German national anthem in 1922.

Bismarck: Prince Otto Eduard Leopold von Bismarck-Schönhausen, Duke of Lauenburg (1815–98), Prime Minister of Prussia from 1862, architect of the German unification of 1871, and subsequently first Chancellor of the Reich. Nietzsche is invariably contemptuous of the leading political figure of his time: in the last piece he wrote, a declaration of 'Deadly War against the House of Hohenzollern', he refers to Bismarck as 'the idiot *par excellence* among all statesmen' (KGW VIII/3, 457).

38 *the two great European narcotics, alcohol and Christianity*: despite his identification with Dionysus, the Greek god of wine, Nietzsche's polemics against the consumption of alcohol, and especially beer, are constant (cf. EH II 1: 'Munich is where my antipodes live'). Although he never read Marx, he comes close here to Marx's famous formulation in the Introduction to the *Critique of Hegel's Philosophy of Right* (1843): 'religion . . . is the opium of the people.'

German music: Wagner is again the implicit target here.

night-gown: a possible allusion to Goethe's *Faust*, Part One, in which Faust's well-meaning but dull pupil (whose name is Wagner!) first enters wearing a night-gown and night-cap.

scholar: despite the section 'We Scholars' in *Beyond Good and Evil*, and his admission in *Ecce Homo*: 'For a time I *had* also to be a scholar' (EH III 'UM' 3), Nietzsche, as here, is generally scathing about erudition and the figure of the scholar, especially the university academic (cf. IX 16).

Once . . . David Strauss: David Friedrich Strauss (1808–74), German writer, prominent exponent of the rationalist critique of religion. In his first *Untimely Meditation, David Strauss the Confessor and the Writer*, Nietzsche had launched a violent attack on Strauss's book *Der alte und der neue Glaube: Ein Bekenntnis* (The Old Faith and the New: A Confession, 1872). Nietzsche generally uses in a pejorative sense the terms 'freethinker' ('Freigeist', as here: cf. IX 2; BGE 44; GM III 24), its French and Italian cognates 'libre penseur' (EH III 'UM' 2; BGE 44) and 'libero pensatoro' (BGE 44), and 'libertin' (IX 3), contrasting them with his own preferred term 'free spirit' ('freier Geist': IV 5; IX 45, 49).

38 *pledged himself... in verse*: allusion to Strauss's poem 'Elegie' (1851), which ends: 'Only death will separate me from my dear brown beer.'

I... German universities: after his retirement on health grounds from Basle University in 1879, Nietzsche lived predominantly in Switzerland, Italy, and France, so his contact with German universities during the 1880s was indeed sporadic, and mostly through his reading of academic publications.

science: 'Wissenschaft', which in German includes both the 'arts' (Geisteswissenschaften) and the 'sciences' (Naturwissenschaften) as academic disciplines.

For seventeen years: i.e. since his attack on (Socratic) 'Wissenschaft' in *The Birth of Tragedy*, and especially his polemics against 'Bildungsphilisterthum' (educated philistinism, Nietzsche's coinage) in the first two *Untimely Meditations*.

or educators: cf. the title of the third *Untimely Meditation*, *Schopenhauer as Educator*.

39 *Europe's flatland*: 'Europa's *Flachland*' develops the opening sentence of this section, on the German mind's 'becoming shallow' ('sich verflacht', literally 'becoming flat'). Nietzsche evidently liked the formulation, reusing it in *Ecce Homo* (III 2) and *Nietzsche contra Wagner* ('Preface'). Cf. also IX 5: 'englisch[e] Flachköpf[e]' (English fat-heads).

sufficient reason: ironic reference to the 'principle of sufficient reason', formulated by the German philosopher Gottfried Wilhelm Leibniz (1646–1716), which states that for every fact there is a reason why it is so and not otherwise. Schopenhauer's doctoral dissertation was *Über die vierfache Wurzel des Satzes vom zureichenden Grunde* (On the Fourfold Root of the Principle of Sufficient Reason, 1813).

self-overcoming: key term in Nietzsche's philosophy. Cf. IX 28, 49; Z II, 'On Self-Overcoming': 'And life itself told me this secret: "Behold," it said, "I am that *which must overcome itself again and again*."'

just a modern idea: Nietzsche's critique of modernity, 'modern men', and especially 'modern ideas' reaches a culmination in *Beyond Good and Evil*, but in *Twilight*, too, he cannot resist making frequent gibes, especially in 'Reconnaissance Raids of an Untimely Man' (cf. IX 2, 18, 37, 39, 41, 48).

Goethe's heart... 'Wars of Liberation': although in *On the Genealogy of Morals* Nietzsche characterizes Napoleon Bonaparte (1769–1821) as a problematic figure, 'this synthesis of the *inhuman* and the *superhuman*' (GM I 16), in *Twilight* his admiration is relatively unalloyed (cf. IX 44–5, 48–9). The 'Wars of Liberation' is the collective term applied to the successful campaign (1813–15) fought by the Prussian armies (in alliance with those of the Russian Tsar) against the forces of Napoleon.

the question of pessimism . . . the question of Wagner: Schopenhauerism and Wagnerism had indeed taken Paris by storm from around 1880 (though whether they were being 'questioned' is a moot point). Wagner is mentioned here for the first time by name (and in all only twice more: IX 4, 30).

Hegel: Georg Wilhelm Friedrich Hegel (1770–1831), leading German idealist philosopher for whom history was the inevitable dialectical progress of self-estranged 'Geist' (cf. note to p. 7) towards a 'return to itself'. Nietzsche is generally hostile to Hegel (and the barbed reference to 'systematists' at I 26 could well be read as an attack on him, the arch-systematist in German philosophy), although his explicit references to Hegel in *Twilight* (here and in a similar list at IX 21) betoken his acknowledgement, at least, of Hegel's importance to the history of philosophy.

40 *Heinrich Heine*: German poet (1797–1856), Nietzsche's favourite (cf. EH II 4: 'The highest conception of the lyric poet was given me by *Heinrich Heine*. . . . It will one day be said that Heine and I have been by far the first artists of the German language').

The fact that . . . amaze: Nietzsche (by this stage, at least) was no longer considering himself a German but a Pole (cf. EH I 3: 'I am a pure-blooded Polish nobleman, in whom there is no drop of bad blood, least of all German').

schooling, education: 'Erziehung, *Bildung*'. 'Bildung', an all-round education in humanistic values ('Humanität') and individualistic self-determination (as in 'Bildungsroman'), had been seen as the object of education in the German-speaking world since the Enlightenment. Nietzsche's attack on contemporary educational values had begun with the five unpublished lectures 'Über die Zukunft unserer Bildungsanstalten' (On the Future of Our Educational Institutions) in 1872, and is further pursued here at IX 29, 47 and X 2.

mature cultures grown sweet: a reprise of the plant metaphor, this time for culture as a fruit growing 'ripe'/'mature' (reif). Cf. V 3 (' "peace of soul" ' as 'the expression of maturity and mastery'), and especially the paragraph between the 'Foreword' and 'Why I Am So Wise' in *Ecce Homo*: 'On this perfect day, when everything has become ripe and not only the grapes are growing brown.'

Jakob [sic] *Burckhardt*: Jacob Burckhardt (1818–97), Swiss historian of art and culture, best known for his *Die Kultur der Renaissance in Italien* (The Civilization of the Renaissance in Italy, 1860). An older colleague of Nietzsche's at Basle University, where they established an enduring friendship. Cf. X 4.

pulchrum est paucorum hominum: 'the beautiful is for the few', quoted from the *Satires* (I. ix. 44) by the Roman poet Horace (Quintus Horatius Flaccus, 65–8 BC).

the democratism of 'education' become 'universal', common: Nietzsche often puns on the words 'allgemein' (general/universal) and 'gemein' (common). His thoroughgoing élitism resurfaces in further attacks on democracy, 'equal rights', and socialism at IX 2, 34, 37–9, 50.

40 *'occupations'... calling*: a pun on the German word 'Beruf', which initially meant a religious 'calling' and was later secularized into 'occupation'/'profession'. The (to a notable extent Nietzsche-inspired) German sociologist Max Weber (1864–1920) charts the shift in his *Die protestantische Ethik und der Geist des Kapitalismus* (The Protestant Ethic and the Spirit of Capitalism, 1904–5).

41 *Learning to see... on all sides*: a definition of Nietzsche's philosophy of 'perspectivism'.

42 *the great Kant*: Kant was (and is) renowned for the relative awkwardness of his style; for Nietzsche, to paraphrase II 3, Kant's stylistic 'ugliness' is 'practically a refutation' of his philosophy.

German grace: 'deutschen Anmuth'. Allusion to the essay 'Über Anmuth und Würde' (On Grace and Dignity, 1793) by the German writer Friedrich Schiller (1759–1805: cf. IX 1).

43 *Reconnaissance Raids*: 'Streifzüge'. 'Streifzug' has primarily military connotations, although it is also used in a transferred sense to mean 'short overview'.

Seneca... toreador of virtue: Lucius Annaeus Seneca (*c*.4 BC–AD 65), Roman Stoic philosopher, tragedian, and statesman, was born in Spain (hence 'toreador'—though perhaps also an ironic reference to the toreador Escamillo in Bizet's opera *Carmen* (1875), which Nietzsche greatly admired (cf. WC 1–3)).

Rousseau: Jean-Jacques Rousseau (1712–78), Swiss political philosopher and writer, herald of the French Revolution and the Romantic movement, another of Nietzsche's favourite antagonists (cf. IX 3, 6, 48). Here Nietzsche is alluding to his call for an abandonment of the supposed advantages of civilization and a return to the life of the 'noble savage', although the slogan 'back to nature!' was not actually his.

in impuris naturalibus: 'in the impurity of nature', an ironic reworking of the phrase *in puris naturalibus* (in the purity of nature), attributed to the Italian medieval philosopher St Thomas Aquinas (1225–74).

the Morality-Trumpeter of Säckingen: an ironic attack on Schiller as arch-representative of 'the *moralizing* tendency in art' (IX 24), by way of a reference to the epic poem by Joseph Viktor von Scheffel (1826–86), *Der Trompeter von Säckingen* (The Trumpeter of Säckingen, 1854), which had been made into a popular opera (1884) by the German composer Victor Nessler (1841–90). Säckingen is in the south-west German region of Swabia, where Schiller was born; 'trumpeter' may also be alluding to his early plans for a military career. Cf. IX 16.

Dante... in graves: Dante Alighieri (1265–1321), Italy's most celebrated poet. A reference to the *Inferno* section of his *Divine Comedy* (1311–21), set in the underworld, with which the hyena is associated in legend.

cant: in English in the original (cf. IX 12; BGE 228: 'that old English vice called *cant*, which is *moral tartuffery*'; and BGE 5: 'The tartuffery ... of old Kant'). Until Kant's father's time, his family name was actually spelt 'Cant'.

intelligible character: cf. note to p. 32 and *On the Genealogy of Morals* (III 12): 'according to Kant, "intelligible character" means that things are constituted in such a way that they are understood only to the extent that the intellect acknowledges them as *completely beyond its grasp*.'

Victor Hugo … nonsense: Victor Hugo (1802–85), French Romantic poet and 'visionary' (hence 'pharos' ('lighthouse'), after the lighthouse on the island of Pharos off Alexandria, one of the wonders of the ancient world). Cf. IX 6.

Liszt: Ferencz (Franz) Liszt (1811–86), Hungarian pianist-composer (and Richard Wagner's father-in-law).

the School of Velocity—after women: Liszt was famous for his pianistic virtuosity, and as a child prodigy had lessons from the Austrian teacher Karl Czerny (1791–1857), composer of the piano studies published as *Die Schule der Geläufigkeit* (The School of Velocity). Nietzsche is also punning here on 'Läufigkeit' (sexual appetite), an allusion to Liszt's equally famous womanizing.

George Sand: pseudonym of Amandine-Aurore-Lucie Dupin, Baroness Dudevant (1804–76), French novelist, dramatist, and travel writer (cf. IX 6).

lactea ubertas: 'milky abundance', a phrase used by the Roman rhetorician Quintilian (*c.* AD 35–*c.*95) to describe the style of the historian Livy (59 BC–AD 17). Nietzsche seems to have been inspired once again by the *Journal des Goncourt* (ii. 25), where (the prolific) Sand is twice described as having the appearance of a 'ruminant'.

'beautiful style': term applied by Winckelmann (cf. note to p. 79) to the characteristic feature of one of the 'principal periods' of Greek art.

Michelet: Jules Michelet (1798–1874), French historian and philosopher, whose *La Révolution française* (The French Revolution, 7 vols., 1847–53) is particularly fervent in its advocacy of republicanism and democracy.

Carlyle: Thomas Carlyle (1795–1881), Scottish writer, another historian of *The French Revolution* (1837), proponent of the view that history is made by 'great men' (*Heroes and Hero-Worship*, 1841). Characterized here as a typical 'dyspeptic' (cf. IX 12, 44; AC 54). In *Ecce Homo*, Nietzsche explicitly rejects the idea that his doctrine of the 'overman' (cf. note to p. 62) might have anything to do with 'the "hero cult" of that great unconscious and involuntary counterfeiter Carlyle' (EH III 1).

John Stuart Mill: English philosopher and social reformer (1806–73), who developed classical English empiricism in the direction of positivism (cf. note to p. 20) with its quest for 'clear', indisputable facts. Cf. note to p. 6.

Les frères de [sic] *Goncourt … Homer*: in their *Journal*, the brothers Goncourt report a number of pejorative remarks made about Homer in Parisian society salons. In Homer's *Iliad*, Ajax the Locrian ('the Lesser Ajax') and Ajax the Telemonian ('the Greater Ajax') are Greek heroes—not brothers, but leaders of the Locrians and Salaminians respectively in the Trojan War.

Offenbach: Jacques Offenbach (1819–80), German-French composer of operettas, among them *La Belle Hélène* (Beautiful Helen, 1864), set during the Trojan War. Although this is the only reference to the composer in Nietzsche's published writings, in a number of notes from the 1880s he praises his musical genius highly, contrasting him with Wagner.

43 *Zola: or 'the joy of stinking'*: Émile Zola (1840–1902), French novelist, principal exponent of French literary Naturalism, which emphasized the determinism of (usually unpleasant) physical surroundings. A double pun, on the title of Zola's novel *La Joie de vivre* (The Joy of Living, 1885) and his own name, which Nietzsche renders in a note from 1881 as 'Gorgon-Zola' (KGW V/2, 474).

Renan: Ernest Renan (1823–92), French rationalist theologian, Orientalist, and writer, who trained as a priest but subsequently turned to academic theology and, like David Strauss, wrote a popular *Life of Jesus* (*Vie de Jésus*, 1863). Nietzsche's attack here is directed more at Renan's *Dialogues philosophiques* (Philosophical Dialogues, 1876), which he read in German translation, and where Renan urges the intellectual élite to assume its 'aristocratic' responsibility for the liberation of man from material oppression through science. His views are also reported in the *Journal des Goncourt*. Cf. IX 6.

la science and la noblesse: 'science and nobility'.

évangile des humbles: 'gospel of the humble' (cf. note to p. 35).

44 *Sainte-Beuve*: Charles-Augustin de Sainte-Beuve (1804–69), French critic, historian, and novelist, who practised an innovative and influential kind of criticism which strove to explicate literary works through detailed psychological portraits of their authors. Nietzsche is again borrowing from the *Journal des Goncourt* here in his characterization.

médisance: 'scandalmongering'.

ressentiment: 'resentment' (cf. note to p. 13).

romantisme: 'Romanticism', a movement which always meets with Nietzsche's criticism (cf. IX 6, 12, 50).

Academy: the Académie française in Paris, founded by Cardinal Richelieu (1585–1642) in 1635, guardian of the 'purity' of the French language.

Port Royal [sic]: Port-Royal des Champs, Cistercian nunnery near Paris which from 1636 to 1710 served as a place of retreat for the persecuted Jansenist heretics, who formed the subject of Sainte-Beuve's six-volume study *Port-Royal* (1840–59).

that famous worm: cf. I 31.

prefigures Baudelaire: Charles Baudelaire (1821–67), French poet, critic, and essayist. Sainte-Beuve himself remarked to Baudelaire on their affinities, as Nietzsche noted when he read the latter's *Œuvres posthumes et Correspondances inédites* (Posthumous Works and Unpublished Correspondence, Paris, 1887).

Imitatio Christi: *De Imitatione Christi* (On the Imitation of Christ, *c*.1414), devotional work ascribed to the German medieval mystic Thomas Hammerken (Thomas à Kempis, 1379/80–1471).

eternal-womanly: allusion to the closing lines of Goethe's *Faust*, Part Two, 'The eternal-womanly | Draws us on', to which Nietzsche often makes ironic allusion (cf. GS, 'Songs of Prince Vogelfrei' 1; WC 6; EH III 5).

that cleverest... to Rome: allusion to the substitute 'humanistic religion' of love, order, and progress which Comte developed in tandem with his positivistic philosophy. Cf. note to p. 20.

'the religion of the heart': ironic allusion to the 'logique du cœur' (logic of the heart), by which Pascal established the heart as the seat of religious feeling.

45 *G. Eliot*: George Eliot, pseudonym of Mary Ann Evans (1819–80), English novelist and translator of Strauss's *Life of Jesus*. Although she abandoned her early Evangelicalism, her writings continued to be strongly influenced by religious concepts of love and duty.

Lettres d'un voyageur: Letters of a Traveller (1837).

46 *Balzac*: Honoré de Balzac (1799–1850), French (Realist!) novelist.

Renan admires her: the fruit of further reading of the *Journal des Goncourt*, where Nietzsche also found Théophile Gautier's observation that Sand had no sooner finished one novel than she started the next.

You must not look at yourself in your experiences: cf. I 35.

'after nature': 'nach der Natur', a translation of the French term 'd'après nature', which occurs, for example, in the Preface to the *Journal des Goncourt*.

camera obscura: 'dark chamber'. A box fitted with a lens, used for projecting an image of an object or landscape on to an internal screen; the forerunner of the photographic 'camera'.

romanciers: 'novelists'.

petits faits: 'little facts' (cf. VIII 6; BGE 28, 34; GM III 24).

47 *Pascal*: cf. note to p. 30.

Raphael: Raffaello Sanzio (1483–1520), Italian painter and architect.

48 *the conceptual opposition... intoxication*: a reference to The Birth of Tragedy, although there only the Dionysian was considered an art of intoxication, the Apollonian being by contrast the art of 'beautiful appearance'.

Music... Dionysian histrionism: this critique of the specialization of music again goes back to The Birth of Tragedy—at which stage, however, Wagner and his 'Gesamtkunstwerk' (total work of art) were heralded as the answer.

the will which removes mountains: cf. 1 Corinthians 13: 2, 'and though I have all faith, so that I could remove mountains, and have not charity, I am nothing'.

49 *the will to power*: crucial term in Nietzsche's philosophy of the 1880s, his ultimate formulation of the 'Dionysian truth' of the world as a seething turmoil of appropriative, life-affirming, mutually opposing forces 'beyond good and evil' (cf. BGE 259; GM II 12; WP 1067: '*This world is the will to power—and nothing besides!* And you yourselves are also this will to power—and nothing besides!'). Elsewhere in *Twilight*, Nietzsche's philosophy of power surfaces

only rarely, at IX 14 ('where there is a struggle, there is a struggle for *power*'), 20, 38, and X 3.

49 *Thomas Carlyle*: cf. note to p. 43.

fettered enough: another buried etymology unearthed, the derivation of 'religion' from the Latin 'religere' ('to bind fast').

proprium: 'characteristic feature'.

cant: again in English in the original (cf. IX 1).

Emerson: Ralph Waldo Emerson (1803–82), American philosopher, essayist, and poet, for whom Nietzsche had a lifelong respect (the first edition of *The Gay Science* had an epigraph by him).

50 *Lope de Vega's*: Lope Félix de Vega Carpio (1562–1635), Spanish poet and dramatist.

'yo me sucedo a mi mismo': 'I am my own heir'. Nietzsche noted the quotation in late 1887, applying it at that stage to himself (KGW VIII/2, 256).

tamquam re bene gesta: 'as though from a successful affair'.

Ut desint vires . . . tamen est laudanda voluptas: 'though the potency be lacking, yet the lust is praiseworthy', a reworking of Ovid, *Epistulae ex Ponto* (Letters from the Black Sea, III. iv. 79), which has 'voluntas' (will) for 'voluptas' (lust).

Anti-Darwin: Charles Robert Darwin (1809–82), English natural historian who transformed biological science with the theory of evolution by 'natural selection', which he expounded in his most (in)famous work, *On the Origin of Species by Means of Natural Selection, or the Preservation of Favoured Races in the Struggle for Life* (1859).

Malthus: Thomas Robert Malthus (1766–1834), English clergyman, economist, and social theorist, who argued in his *Essay on the Principle of Population* (1798) that whereas population increases exponentially, the means of subsistence increase only arithmetically, with the result that, failing moral restraint, population can be kept in check only through famine, disease, and war.

Species . . . cleverer: cf. note to p. 15 and GM I 10: 'A race of such men of resentment is bound in the end to become *cleverer* than any noble race, and it will respect cleverness to a completely different degree.'

'let it go! . . . for the Reich must still be ours': ironic quotations from 'Ein' feste Burg ist unser Gott' ('A strong fortress is our God')—the most famous hymn by Martin Luther (1483–1546), leader of the Protestant Reformation in Germany—where it is the things of this world that are to be 'let go', and the 'Reich' is the kingdom of heaven.

mimicry: in English in the original, a key survival strategy in Darwinian biology.

51 *'impersonal' type*: cf. IX 28, where 'The "impersonal" have a chance to speak'.

'Goethe and Schiller': Germany's 'G and S'. The close and artistically productive friendship between the two greatest writers of German literary classicism lasted from 1794 till Schiller's death in 1805, and has been celebrated since.

Hartmann: Eduard von Hartmann (1842–1906), German philosopher, one of Nietzsche's targets since *On the Use and Disadvantage of History for Life* (UM II 9), on account of his synthesis of Hegelian historicism and Schopenhauerian pessimism.

52 *actors*: cf. I 38; X 3. The histrionic talent of Wagner in particular is an important theme in Nietzsche's polemics against his '*décadence*' (cf. WC 8–9; NcW, 'Where I Offer Objections').

'beautiful in itself': (Platonic) idea of beauty in the abstract; here an allusion to Kant's separation of beauty from the realms of utility, pleasure, and goodness in his *Kritik der Urteilskraft* (Critique of Judgement, 1790).

man . . . the measure of perfection: allusion to the maxim 'man is the measure of all things' (quoted in Plato's *Theaetetus*, 160d) by the Greek philosopher Protagoras of Abdera (*c*.481–411 BC).

sublimities: a word which manages in this context to conflate both the sensation of the 'sublime' (cf. IV 3) and the 'sublimation' of the instincts (cf. HA I 1).

53 *Ariadne . . . Naxos*: in Greek mythology, Bacchus (Dionysus) successfully woos Ariadne on the island of Naxos after she has been abandoned there by her former lover Theseus.

I find . . . even longer: cf. EH III 2: 'We all know . . . what a longears is. Very well, I dare to assert that I possess the smallest ears. . . . I am the *anti-ass par excellence*.'

'ugly'. A hatred: in German, 'hässlich' (ugly) and 'Hass' (hatred) are etymologically related.

nihilistic devaluation of all life: for 'nihilism', cf. note to p. 9. The 'denial of the will to life' is for Schopenhauer, heavily influenced by the Buddhistic concept of 'nirvana', the path to salvation from the ills of the world (cf. *The World as Will and Representation*, i. 68). Cf. X 4 on the Greek affirmation of the 'will to life'.

54 *sexuality*: cf. *The World as Will and Representation*, Books 2 and 3.

divine Plato . . . calls him: cf. Schopenhauer's *On the Fourfold Root of the Principle of Sufficient Reason*, i. 1 and Preface to the first edition of *The World as Will and Representation*.

all beauty stimulates procreation: cf. Plato, *Symposium*, 206b–d.

he says . . . beautiful soil: cf. Plato, *Phaedrus*, 249c–256e.

amor intellectualis dei: 'intellectual love of God', a term from Spinoza's *Ethics* (V, Prop. 32, Coroll.).

conceptual cobwebbery . . . Spinoza: Nietzsche often uses the metaphor of the spider in the context of Spinoza, punning on the German for spider (Spinne) and mocking the rationalistic, 'geometrical' method of Spinoza's *Ethics* (cf. note to p. 18).

55 *Philosophy . . . dialectics*: cf. II 8.

55 *L'art pour l'art*: 'art for art's sake', a slogan coined in 1818 by the French philosopher and politician Victor Cousin (1792–1867) and adopted as an aesthetic creed by many writers of the later nineteenth century, especially in France (Baudelaire, Flaubert) and England (the 'aesthetic' movement).

a worm biting its own tail: an image parodying the ancient symbol of the 'uroborus', a snake biting its own tail, which Nietzsche himself used as a symbol of the eternal return (cf. note to p. 80).

Art is the great stimulant to life: this assertion and the rest of the paragraph echo the argument of *The Birth of Tragedy*.

'freeing oneself from the will' . . . tragedy: cf. *The World as Will and Representation*, Book 3, especially 51.

56 *Saturnalia*: 'festival of Saturn' held every December in ancient Rome, in which the merry-making extended unusually even to slaves, who were served by their masters for a day. Cf. HA II 220; GS, 'Preface' 1.

merely liberal: for a more sustained critique of liberalism and liberal institutions, cf. IX 38.

middling, communicable things: 'Mittleres, Mittheilsames'. Cf. GS 354, where Nietzsche argues that language, and consciousness itself, developed '*only under the pressure of the need for communication*'.

'This portrait is enchantingly beautiful!': the title of Tamino's aria in Act I of Mozart's opera *Die Zauberflöte* (The Magic Flute, 1791).

'aut liberi aut libri': 'either children or books'.

57 *'je me verrai . . . tant d'esprit?'*: 'I shall see myself, read myself, go into ecstasies and say: could I possibly have been so witty?' Quoted from a letter of the Italian economist and writer Ferdinando Galiani (1728–87) to Mme d'Épinay (1725–83), 18 September 1869.

Doctoral Viva: oral examination of a doctoral candidate, held on completion of his (in Nietzsche's time) dissertation.

the concept of duty: given its highest philosophical expression in the philosophy of Kant (cf. *Critique of Practical Reason*), which also establishes the duality of 'thing in itself' and 'appearance', mocked again at the end of this paragraph (cf. note to p. 19).

The weary . . . go their own way: Nietzsche returns to 'the labour question' at IX 34, 40, and to a critique of *laisser-aller*/'letting oneself go' at IX 41, 47.

classes: 'Klassen'. 'Klasse' is a word Nietzsche very rarely uses, preferring 'Schichte' (stratum: IX 34), 'Stand' (station: IX 37), or 'Rang' (rank/rate: III 4).

'nodding wild drives' . . . Faust: reference to Goethe's *Faust*, Part One: 'Wild drives are nodding now' (l. 1182).

58 *Bayreuth*: Richard Wagner's 'headquarters' in northern Bavaria, site of the 'Festspielhaus' in which his music dramas were (and continue to be) performed at an annual summer festival.

pure folly: ironic allusion to Wagner's last work, the 'stage-consecrating festival play' *Parsifal* (1882), whose hero is described as a 'pure [i.e. morally untainted] fool'.

Another Problem of Diet: i.e. after the problem of 'Cornarism' discussed at VI 1.

Julius Caesar: Gaius Julius Caesar (100–44 BC), Roman Emperor and general. Nietzsche's source for this characterization of Caesar was the same as Shakespeare's for his *Julius Caesar*, the *Parallel Lives* by the Greek biographer Plutarch (*c.* AD 46–*c.*120).

partie honteuse: 'shameful part'.

59 *illnesses ... the causes of it*: cf. VI 2.

Christian and Anarchist: cf. AC 58: 'One may assert an absolute equivalence between *Christian* and *anarchist*.' For 'anarchist', cf. also I 36.

canaille: 'riff-raff'.

60 *socialists*: Nietzsche's conflation of anarchism and socialism here is typical (cf. GM I 5).

61 *a death which is not free*: 'Freitod' (free death) is the German for suicide.

We have no power ... a mistake: cf. the wisdom of Silenus at BT 3: 'What is best of all is utterly beyond your reach: not to be born, not to *be*, to be *nothing*. But the second best for you is—to die soon.'

pur, vert: 'pure, green'.

62 *'will and representation'*: cf. Schopenhauer, *The World as Will and Representation* (1819/44).

Cesare Borgia: Italian general, cardinal, and political machinator (1474/6–1507), Machiavelli's model for *The Prince* (cf. note to p. 77). In *Beyond Good and Evil* (197) Nietzsche characterizes him as a 'man of prey' and 'tropical monster' who must not be discredited 'for the benefit of "temperate zones"'; here and in *The Antichrist*, where he considers the prospect of '*Cesare Borgia as Pope*' 'a *possibility* of a quite unearthly fascination and splendour' (61), he is evidently more fulsome in his admiration. Cf. also AC 46; EH III 1.

'higher man' ... overman: the 'overman' (Übermensch) is one of Nietzsche's key figures who makes his only appearance in *Twilight* here. He is defined in *Ecce Homo* as 'a type that has turned out supremely well, in antithesis to "modern" men, to "good" men, to Christians and other nihilists' (EH III 1): producing the overman is the goal of the self-overcoming of humanity; he is 'beyond good and evil', the embodiment of Nietzsche's 'philosophy of the future'. In a long section in Book IV of *Thus Spake Zarathustra*, though ('Of the Higher Man'), Nietzsche is careful to distinguish between the 'higher men' who prepare the way, and the advent of the overman himself.

A Swiss editor ... Bund: *Bund* was a daily newspaper published in Berne; its book-review section was edited by Josef Viktor Widmann (1842–1911), who reviewed *Beyond Good and Evil* in 1886. Nietzsche refers to the incident again at EH III 1.

Much obliged!: 'Sehr verbunden!', a pun on the title of the newspaper.

62 *the men of the Renaissance*: what Nietzsche admires about 'Renaissance men' *à la* Cesare Borgia or Machiavelli (cf. X 2) is not so much their 'virtuosity' as their very concept of 'virtue' as *virtù* (manliness). He returns to the Renaissance as a great period in history at IX 44, 49.

63 *l'impressionisme* [sic] *morale*: 'moral impressionism'. The term *impressionniste* was coined in 1874 by the Parisian art critic Leroy to describe the first exhibition of 'Impressionist' paintings, and was soon both adopted by the group of artists themselves and applied in other fields, as here.

Schopenhauer's morality of sympathy: cf. *The World as Will and Representation*, ii. 47 ('On Ethics'): '*sympathy or compassion*, which is, as I have shown, the basis of justice and philanthropy, *caritas*'.

attempt: 'Versuch', which also means 'experiment'.

'loving one's neighbour': cf. I 9 and Z I, 'Of Love of One's Neighbour'.

64 *'Equality'... decline*: further developed in the next two paragraphs, at IX 48 ('never make the unequal equal'), and especially AC 43: 'The poison of the doctrine "*equal* rights for all"—this has been more thoroughly sown by Christianity than by anything else.'

pathos of distance: a term encapsulating Nietzsche's politics, on which he elaborates at BGE 257: 'the *pathos of distance* such as develops from the incarnate differences of classes ['Stände', as here], from the ruling caste's constant looking out and looking down on subjects and instruments and from its equally constant exercise of obedience and command, its holding down and holding at a distance' (cf. GM I 2, III 14; AC 43).

Mr Herbert Spencer: English philosopher and sociologist (1820–1903), proponent of what became known as 'social Darwinism', a theory which applied principles taken from Darwinian biology to socio-economic analysis, and can be summed up in the phrase (which Spencer coined) 'the survival of the fittest'.

herd animal: cf. BGE 202 and 199: 'ever since there have been human beings there have also been human herds (family groups, communities, tribes, nations, states, churches), and always very many who obey compared with the very small number of those who command.'

65 *Human, All Too Human*: Nietzsche gives a page reference to the first German edition, which corresponds to paragraph 472 in the section 'A Glance at the State': 'modern democracy is the historical form of the *decay of the state*.' Cf. also BGE 203.

66 *imperium Romanum*: 'Roman empire'.

67 *the European worker... turned into a question*: 'Arbeiter-Frage' (labour question) means literally 'the question of the workers'.

'Freedom as I do not mean it...': a parody of 'Freedom, as I mean it', the opening line of the poem 'Freiheit' (Freedom) by the German poet Max von Schenkendorf (1783–1817).

68 *in politicis*: 'in political matters'.

a different kind of saint: i.e. 'wunderliche Heilige' (strange fellows), literally 'strange/wondrous saints'—the description Nietzsche has already applied in this section to Schopenhauer (IX 22) and Plato (IX 23).

truths of practical reason: ironic reference to Kant's *Critique of Practical Reason*, in which he discusses the grounds for moral action.

Procrustean bed: Polypemon, or Procrustes (Greek for 'stretcher') was a legendary Greek robber who would lay travellers on his bed, and if they were too long for it he would cut their limbs shorter; if they were too short he would stretch them to make them fit.

crab-like retrogression...free to be a crab: cf. I 24.

69 *Great men [...] explosions*: this notion of 'explosivity' (cf. VI 4; X 3) is developed repeatedly elsewhere (cf. UM III 8; GM III 15: 'that most dangerous explosive substance, *resentment*'), especially in *Ecce Homo* (cf. EH III 'UM' 3; IV 1: 'I am not a man, I am dynamite').

the theory of milieu: the theory that one's surroundings ('milieu') are more important than heredity in the formation of one's character. Its main exponents were Auguste Comte (cf. note to p. 20 and IX 4) and the French historian Hippolyte Taine (1828–93), whose praise Nietzsche courted, but whom he nevertheless criticized for having been corrupted by Hegelianism (cf. EH II 3).

Buckle: Henry Thomas Buckle (1821–62), English cultural historian, whom Nietzsche also criticizes in *On the Genealogy of Morals* (I 4) as an example of 'the *plebeian nature* of the modern mind'.

70 *Dostoevsky*: Fyodor Mikhailovich Dostoevsky (1821–81), Russian novelist. The reference here is to *Notes from the House of the Dead* (1860–2), his account of his experiences in prison in Omsk.

Stendhal: pseudonym of Henri Beyle (1783–1842), French writer. Cf. BGE 254; EH II 3: 'Stendhal...is utterly invaluable with his anticipating psychologist's eye, with his grasp of facts...; finally not least as an *honest* atheist.... Perhaps I am even envious of Stendhal?'

71 *Chandala*: cf. VII 3–4.

So long...devalued: the reign of the 'ascetic priest' is one of the central topics analysed in the Third Essay of *On the Genealogy of Morals* (15–22).

'Catilinarian existence': Catiline (Lucius Sergius Catilina, 108–62 BC), Roman politician who led two unsuccessful coup attempts (65, 63 BC) before being forced to flee Rome; seen by Nietzsche here as a precursor of Caesar, whose successful coup took place in 49 BC. The phrase 'Catilinarian existence' was used initially by Bismarck, in a pejorative sense.

all that already is and no longer becomes: cf. III 1.

Here the View is Clear: quotation from the closing scene of Goethe's *Faust*, Part Two (l. 11989).

'il est indigne...qu'ils ressentent': 'it is unworthy of great souls to spread the inner turmoil they feel.'

71 *greatness of soul*: an Aristotelian term (*megalopsychia*: cf. *Nicomachean Ethics*, iv. 3).

became: 'ward'. Nietzsche deliberately chooses the archaic preterite form used in Luther's Bible translation.

72 *seventeenth-century France*: a period which ranks almost as highly as classical Greece and Renaissance Italy in Nietzsche's hierarchy of cultures (cf. IX 23).

Christianity, which has despised the body: cf. Z I, 'Of the Despisers of the Body'; AC 21: 'Here the body is despised, hygiene repudiated as sensuality; the Church even resists cleanliness.'

'return to nature': cf. note to p. 43.

73 *in rebus tacticis*: 'in tactical matters'.

The doctrine of equality: cf. the French Revolutionary slogan 'liberté, égalité, fraternité' (liberty, equality, fraternity). Nietzsche's most powerful attack on the 'will to equality' is the section 'Of the Tarantulas' in *Thus Spake Zarathustra*, II: 'you preachers of *equality*! You are tarantulas and dealers in hidden revengefulness!'

practical activity above all: cf. the quotation from Goethe's letter to Schiller of 19 December 1798 with which Nietzsche begins the Foreword to the second *Untimely Meditation*: 'In any case, I hate everything that merely instructs me without augmenting or directly invigorating my activity.'

74 *ens realissimum*: cf. note to p. 18.

he no longer denies ... Dionysus: cf. note to p. 19.

a reverence for everything actual: cf. Nietzsche's praise for Thucydides on this account at X 2, but also IX 7: 'Seeing *what there is*—that goes with a different kind of mind, the *anti-artistic*, factual mind.'

in praxi: 'in practice'.

75 *three things ... the 'cross'*: allusion to the sixty-sixth of Goethe's *Venezianische Epigramme* (Venetian Epigrams, 1786–8), where he lists his four pet hates: tobacco smoke, bugs, garlic, and the (Christian) cross.

nowhere am I worse read than in my fatherland: cf. EH III 2 and NcW, 'Foreword': 'I have my readers everywhere, in Vienna, in St Petersburg, in Copenhagen and Stockholm, in Paris, in New York—I do *not* have them in Europe's flatland, Germany.'

the most independent one: i.e. the 'Revaluation of All Values'.

76 *Sallust*: Gaius Sallustius Crispus (86–35 BC), Roman writer and historian who took Thucydides as his model and was noted for his terseness (Quintilian writes of his 'famous brevity').

Corssen: Wilhelm Corssen (1820–75), classical philologist who taught at Pforta, the school Nietzsche attended from 1858 to 1864.

'aere perennius': 'more everlasting than bronze', quoted from Horace, *Odes*, III. xxx. 1. Cf. 'The Hammer Speaks' (XI).

Horace: cf. note to p. 40.

77 *Plato ... stylistic décadent*: in *Ecce Homo* Nietzsche boasts of his own 'manifold art of style' (EH III 4), but his point here is that, unlike himself—or Thucydides, at the end of this paragraph—Plato is not in control of his stylistic diversity.

Cynics: school of Greek philosophers founded in Athens by Antisthenes (*c*.445–*c*.360 BC), a pupil and friend of Socrates, its most famous adherent being Diogenes of Sinope (*c*.400–325 BC), nicknamed 'the dog' (*kuon*, hence the group's name) on account of his contempt for convention and shameless flouting of public morality.

satura Menippea: 'Menippean satire', genre named after Menippus of Gadara (third century BC), a Cynic philosopher who satirized contemporary folly in a mixture of prose and verse. None of his writings survive, but Marcus Terentius Varro (116–27 BC) imitated his style in his *Saturae Menippeae*.

Fontenelle: Bernhard Le Bovier de Fontenelle (1657–1757), French philosopher, writer, and scientific popularizer. His *Nouveaux Dialogues des morts* (New Dialogues of the Dead, 1683), in particular, established his reputation for wit and stylistic elegance.

proto-Christian: in so far as the development of Christianity itself was so influenced by the Neoplatonic doctrines of Plotinus (*c*. AD 205–70), Porphyry (*c*. AD 232–305), and the later (fifth- and sixth-century) Alexandrian school.

this Athenian ... the Jews in Egypt: according to legend (for there is no biographical material to substantiate the claim) Plato's remarks on Egypt (e.g. the opening of the *Timaeus*) are based on personal experience.

Thucydides: Greek historian (*c*.460–*c*.400 BC), whose much-admired *History of the Peloponnesian War* describes the greater part of the conflict between Athens and Sparta for dominance in Greece, 431–404 BC.

Macchiavell's [sic] *principe*: Niccolò Machiavelli, Florentine politician and writer (1469–1527), best known for his study of 'Machiavellian' statecraft, *Il principe* (The Prince, 1513).

Sophistic: 'Sophist' (from *sophia*, 'wisdom') was the term applied in Athens from the middle of the fifth century BC to those who gave lessons for money in rhetoric, politics, and mathematics (denounced by Plato in his *Sophist* and many of the other dialogues).

Socratic schools: various schools of philosophy founded in ancient Greece by pupils of Socrates, including not only Plato's Academy and the Cynic school of Antisthenes, but the Megarian school of Eucleides of Megara (*fl. c*.390 BC) and the Cyrenaic school of Aristippus of Cyrene.

78 *'beautiful souls'*: term from Winckelmann (cf. note to p. 79) popularized by Goethe's novel *Wilhelm Meisters Lehrjahre* (Wilhelm Meister's Apprenticeship, 1795), Book 6 of which is entitled 'Confessions of a Beautiful Soul'.

repose in greatness ... lofty naïvety: allusion to the essay 'Gedanken über die Nachahmung der Griechischen Werke in der Malerei und Bildhauerkunst' (Thoughts on the Imitation of Greek Works in Painting and Sculpture, 1755) by Winckelmann, in which he formulates an idealized image of the 'noble naïvety and the tranquil greatness' (79) of Greek art.

78 *niaiserie allemande*: 'German inanity'.

They came...from the start: cf. IX 47: 'Even the beauty of a race or a family, its grace and goodness in all its gestures, is worked for.'

agonal instinct: cf. note to p. 14.

polis: ancient Greek political unit of the city state.

79 *I was...an excess of strength*: the reference here is, once more, to *The Birth of Tragedy*. Cf. also 'Foreword': 'Excess of strength is the sole proof of strength.'

Jakob Burckhardt: cf. note to p. 40.

Culture of the Greeks: a book which did not yet exist. Nietzsche had attended some of Burckhardt's lectures on the subject during his time at Basle, and possessed copies of two full sets of lecture notes made by students of his. The lectures were eventually published posthumously, as *Griechische Kultur-geschichte* (Greek Cultural History, 1930–1).

Lobeck: Christian August Lobeck (1781–1860), German classical philologist.

Aglaophamus: Lobeck's principal work (2 vols., 1829), on the ancient mystery cults.

Winckelmann: Johann Joachim Winckelmann (1717–68), German archaeologist and historian of ancient art, one of Goethe's early influences.

80 *eternal return*: 'the unconditional and endlessly repeated circular course of all things' (EH III 'BT' 3), one of Nietzsche's central ideas which he first formulates in *Thus Spake Zarathustra* (cf. Z III, 'The Convalescent'). He in fact uses two synonyms interchangeably: 'ewige Wiederkehr' (as here) and 'ewige Wiederkunft' (as at the end of the next paragraph, where it is translated as 'eternal recurrence').

For the eternal joy of creation...exist eternally: cf. Z II, 'On the Blissful Islands': 'For the creator himself to be the child new-born he must also be willing to be the mother and endure the mother's pain.'

Dionysia: various Athenian festivals held in honour of Dionysus which included sacrifices and dramatic performances as well as the tasting of the new wine, the parading of sculpted phalluses, symbolic marriages, and orgies.

resentment: cf. note to p. 13.

81 *freeing oneself...Aristotle's understanding of it*: Aristotle's definition of emotional *catharsis* ('purging') as the purpose of tragedy (*Poetics*, 6).

the joy of destruction: cf. Z II, 'Of Self-Overcoming': 'And he who has to be a creator in good and evil, truly, has first to be a destroyer and break values' (quoted at EH IV 2). Cf. also XI.

I, the last disciple of the philosopher Dionysus: cf. note to p. 19. A similar declaration of Dionysianism occurs in the penultimate paragraph of another of Nietzsche's works, *Beyond Good and Evil* (BGE 295).

82 *Thus Spake Zarathustra, III*: this whole passage is a slightly modified version of 'Of Old and New Law-Tables', 29. The peculiar poetic, mock-biblical style of *Zarathustra* is evident even from this short extract, in which there are three examples of wordplay in the German: 'soft'/'yielding' (weich/weichend); 'denial'/'disavowal' (Leugnung/Verleugnung); and 'cut'/'cleave' (schneiden/zerschneiden).

harder than bronze: i.e. '*aere perennius*'. Cf. note to p. 76.

noblest: 'Edelste', a pun on the German for 'precious stone', 'Edelstein' (literally, 'noble stone').

INDEX

For ease of use, cross-references within major semantic fields have been grouped under the following entries: animal; art; body; education; happiness; health; language; plant; politics; power; religion; time; war.

post-structuralism xxiv, xxviii

power xx, xxxiii, 29, 37, 39, 47–50, 53, 59, 66; *see also* ability; authority; commanding; discipline; dominance; effort; energy; force; imperative; impotence; inability; law; master; measure; muscle; obedience; order; organization; overcoming; overman; poor; possession; privilege; punishment; rich; rule; selection; self-control; slave; strong; subject; subordination; system; weak; will to power

practical reason 68, 107

pregnancy 80

pride 21, 49, 53, 61

priest(s) xxx–xxxi, 22, 25, 26, 31, 33–4, 36, 43, 68, 71–2, 79, 107

privilege 30, 35, 40, 50, 59

procreation xxxiii, 16, 54, 61, 80

Procrustes 68, 107

profundity 3, 8, 22, 38, 53, 61, 63, 70, 75, 79–80

progress xxxiv, 20, 62–3, 68, 72

projection 18, 28, 51, 90

promise 20, 66, 71

Protagoras 103

psychology/psychologist xviii–xx, xxii–xxiii, xxvi, xxviii–xxix, xxxii–xxxiii, 3, 5, 9, 17, 18, 28–31, 36, 39, 44, 46–7, 50–1, 53–5, 65, 70, 78, 80–1, 107; *see also* Geist; idleness of a psychologist; soul

punishment 30–2, 94

pure/purity 35, 43, 58, 80, 105

purpose 31–2, 55

Pütz, Peter xv

quiet 3, 15, 23, 71

Quintilian 99, 108

rabble 12, 13, 87

race xxx, 27, 34, 72

Raphael 47, 101

rational(ity) 14–15, 34, 66, 67; *see also* reason

raven 11

reaction 22, 41, 48, 53

reader/reading ix–x, xi–xii, xix, xxiii–xxiv, xxvii, xxxv, 26, 27, 37, 38, 42, 45, 49, 58, 75, 77, 108; *see also* book; magazines; newspaper

real(ity) 3, 16–17, 19, 24, 27, 28, 33, 46, 58, 62, 77–8; *see also* ens realissimum

realism/realist 74, 77–8

real world xxvii, xxix, 16–17, 19, 20

reason xv, xxvi, 12, 14–15, 16–19, 20, 25, 26–7, 39, 43, 67, 74, 77, 90; *see also* practical reason; rational

reason(ing) 12, 13, 16, 19, 24, 26, 29, 30, 38, 45, 50, 57, 71, 73, 78, 79; *see also* explanation; justification; sufficient reason

rebellion 71

recovery 5, 39, 87

recuperation x, xxv, 3, 77

redemption 20, 32, 54, 74; *see also* deliverance; relief; saviour

Reich xvii, 22, 39–40, 50, 57, 64–6, 85, 95, 102

relief 29, 34

religion 12, 23, 26, 30–1, 33–5, 44, 60, 69, 80, 95, 102; *see also* atheist; Bible; Buddhism; Catholic; Christian; church; Devil; disciple; divine service; Enoch; faith; fetishism; God; god; gospel; Hinduism; idol; Jesuit; Jew; Manu; metaphysics; monastery; monotono-theism; piety; priest; saint; scepticism; theology; worship; Zoroastrianism

remorse xxv, 6, 8, 85–6

Renaissance 62–3, 69, 73, 106, 108

Renan, Ernest xviii, 43, 46, 94, 100

repentance 20

representation 9, 16, 28, 48, 62; *see also* imitation; mime; mimic; symbol

repression xxviii

resentment xxx, 13, 44, 80, 88, 107

resistance 27, 41, 44, 65, 86

respect(able) 13, 16, 45, 58, 62, 65, 73, 79; *see also* self-respect

responsibility 3, 27, 31–2, 61, 64, 66–7, 94

ressentiment, see resentment

restoration 27, 58

retroaction xxix–xxx, 24, 28–9, 93

retrogression 68

revaluation of all values 3, 26, 35, 81, 83

revealing 13, 55, 78, 85, 88

revenge xxx, 13, 19, 21, 35, 44, 59–60, 71, 88, 108

reverence xxxiv, 17, 23, 74–5

	Classical Literary Criticism
	Greek Lyric Poetry
	Myths from Mesopotamia
Apollodorus	**The Library of Greek Mythology**
Apollonius of Rhodes	**Jason and the Golden Fleece**
Apuleius	**The Golden Ass**
Aristotle	**The Nicomachean Ethics** **Physics** **Politics**
Caesar	**The Civil War** **The Gallic War**
Catullus	**The Poems of Catullus**
Cicero	**The Nature of the Gods**
Euripides	**Medea, Hippolytus, Electra, and Helen**
Galen	**Selected Works**
Herodotus	**The Histories**
Hesiod	**Theogony and Works and Days**
Homer	**The Iliad** **The Odyssey**
Horace	**The Complete Odes and Epodes**
Juvenal	**The Satires**
Livy	**The Rise of Rome**
Lucan	**The Civil War**
Marcus Aurelius	**The Meditations**
Ovid	**The Love Poems** **Metamorphoses** **Sorrows of an Exile**

The Oxford World's Classics Website

www.worldsclassics.co.uk

- Information about new titles
- Explore the full range of Oxford World's Classics
- Links to other literary sites and the main OUP webpage
- Imaginative competitions, with bookish prizes
- Peruse *Compass*, the Oxford World's Classics magazine
- Articles by editors
- Extracts from Introductions
- A forum for discussion and feedback on the series
- Special information for teachers and lecturers

www.worldsclassics.co.uk

American Literature

British and Irish Literature

Children's Literature

Classics and Ancient Literature

Colonial Literature

Eastern Literature

European Literature

History

Medieval Literature

Oxford English Drama

Poetry

Philosophy

Politics

Religion

The Oxford Shakespeare

A complete list of Oxford Paperbacks, including Oxford World's Classics, OPUS, Past Masters, Oxford Authors, Oxford Shakespeare, Oxford Drama, and Oxford Paperback Reference, is available in the UK from the Academic Division Publicity Department, Oxford University Press, Great Clarendon Street, Oxford OX2 6DP.

In the USA, complete lists are available from the Paperbacks Marketing Manager, Oxford University Press, 198 Madison Avenue, New York, NY 10016.

Oxford Paperbacks are available from all good bookshops. In case of difficulty, customers in the UK can order direct from Oxford University Press Bookshop, Freepost, 116 High Street, Oxford OX1 4BR, enclosing full payment. Please add 10 per cent of published price for postage and packing.